Teatime
SCONES

JASMINE GREEN TEA SCONES,
page 48

Teatime
SCONES

A cherished collection of time-honored recipes

83PRESS

83 PRESS

Copyright ©2023 by Hoffman Media

Hoffman Media
2323 2nd Avenue North
Birmingham, Alabama 35203
hoffmanmedia.com

ISBN #978-0-9835984-8-0
Printed in China

ON THE COVER:
(Front Cover) Bacon-Butternut Gluten-free Scones, page 120; "Everything" Scones, page 76; Pineapple, Macadamia & Coconut Dairy-free Scones, page 101; Strawberry, Lavender & White Chocolate Scones, page 49; Sultana-Buttermilk Scones, page 27.
(Back Cover) New Zealand Cheddar Scones, page 83.

EUROPEAN BUTTER SCONES,
page 17

MIXED BERRY &
THYME SCONES,
page 33

Contents

Introduction

IT IS SAID THAT THE SCOTS WERE THE INVENTORS OF SCONES—pronounced *skahnz* or *skownz*, depending on one's provenance—in the early 16th century. Those first scones were made of oat flour and were cut into wedges and then baked. When the ritual of afternoon tea caught on during the Victorian era of the late 19th century, scones became requisite. These iconic bakes have long been part of traditional afternoon tea; though, whether their proper place is as a first course (American style) or as a second course (British style) is certainly cause for great debate. A cream tea, however, consists of just one course—scones with clotted cream and jam, accompanied by a cup of hot tea—and that is precisely what *Teatime Scones* celebrates.

This collection of 100 favorite recipes for scones from the test kitchens of *TeaTime* magazine lauds the vast array of variations possible. Divided into plain, sweet, savory, and allergy-friendly chapters, there is something for virtually every palate and dietary need, including gluten-free, dairy-free, low-carb, and diabetic. Although most scones served for teatime tend to be round nowadays, other shaped cutters can be employed to convey a particular theme for the occasion, adding unexpected charm to a baked good that might otherwise have a plain appearance. The dough takes well to myriad additions that impart flavorful, if not visual, interest, such as fresh or dried fruits, cheeses, nuts, chocolate, herbs, and much more, as the recipe index on page 133 will confirm. Since experienced bakers insist that the key to a successful scone is a light touch, beginners will find the pictorial how-to that starts on page 129 to be of great help in perfecting their technique.

While purchased clotted cream and a favorite prepared jam or marmalade are the typical condiments for scones, the spreads chapter, which begins on page 121, presents 19 recipes for alternate toppings that are sure to delight as well. Aside from knowing the best spreads to complement the taste of the scone, selecting the best tea to go with the treat is of utmost importance. The "Tea-Pairing Guide" on page 11 suggests infusions that work with some of the main flavor categories found in this book, while the "Tea-Steeping Guide" on page 10 provides step-by-step guidance for making a great pot of hot tea.

Whether enjoyed as just a cream tea or as part of a full afternoon tea, scones continue to be in style, having endured for many centuries and hopefully many more to come.

ALMOND
SUGAR-FREE SCONES,
page 109

TEA-STEEPING *Guide*

The quality of the tea served at afternoon tea is as important as the food and the décor. To be sure your infusion is successful every time, here are some basic guidelines to follow.

WATER

Always use the best water possible. If the water tastes good, so will your tea. Heat the water on the stove top or in an electric kettle to the desired temperature. A microwave oven is not recommended.

TEMPERATURE

Heating the water to the correct temperature is arguably one of the most important factors in making a pot of great tea. Pouring boiling water on green, white, or oolong tea leaves can result in a very unpleasant brew. Always refer to the tea purveyor's packaging for specific instructions, but in general, use 170° to 195° water for these delicate tea types. Reserve boiling (212°) water for black and puerh teas, as well as herbal and fruit tisanes.

TEAPOT

If the teapot you plan to use is delicate, warm it with hot tap water first to avert possible cracking. Discard this water before adding the tea leaves or tea bags.

TEA

Use the highest-quality tea you can afford, whether loose leaf or prepackaged in bags or sachets. Remember that these better teas can often be steeped more than once. When using loose-leaf tea, generally use 1 generous teaspoon of dry leaf per 8 ounces of water, and use an infuser basket. For a stronger infusion, add another teaspoonful or two of dry tea leaf.

TIME

As soon as the water reaches the correct temperature for the type of tea, pour it over the leaves or tea bag in the teapot, and cover the pot with a lid. Set a timer—usually 1 to 2 minutes for whites and oolongs; 2 to 3 minutes for greens; and 3 to 5 minutes for blacks, puerhs, and herbals. (Steeping tea longer than recommended can yield a bitter infusion.) When the timer goes off, remove the infuser basket or the tea bags from the teapot.

ENJOYMENT

For best flavor, serve the tea as soon as possible. Keep the beverage warm atop a lighted warmer or under your favorite tea cozy if necessary.

TEA-PAIRING *Guide*

Selecting a tea that perfectly complements the scone with which it is served is of utmost importance. When choosing an infusion, the flavor of the tea should enhance—rather than compete with or overpower—the taste and mouthfeel of these teatime treats. Because white teas are quite delicate, they are best reserved for drinking on their own instead of pairing them with food. Greens, blacks, and most oolongs are excellent choices for serving alongside this beloved teatime course. Following are a few recommendations for the various flavor profiles of the scones in this book:

AUTUMN SPICES Nepal Ilam Black Tea, Assam Belseri Black Tea, Nilgiri Frost Black Tea

BERRIES Jasmine Green Tea, Darjeeling 2nd Flush Black Tea, China Milk Oolong Tea

CHEESE Assam Golden Tips Black Tea, Bohea Black Tea, Gunpowder Green Tea

CHOCOLATE Keemun Spring Mao Feng Black Tea, most fruit-flavored black teas

CITRUS Darjeeling Ambootia Black Tea, Fujian Ti Kuan Yin Oolong Tea, Earl Grey Black Tea

DRIED FRUITS Golden Monkey Black Tea, Ceylon Kenilworth Estate Black Tea, Colombian Black Tea

FLORAL Darjeeling 1st Flush Black Tea, Nilgiri Black Tea, Formosa Oolong Tea

HERBS Ceylon Lover's Leap Estate Black Tea, Dragonwell Green Tea, Sencha Green Tea

NUTS Nepal Mist Valley Black Tea, Da Hong Pao Oolong Tea, most spice-flavored black teas

OLIVES Gyokuro Green Tea, Colombian Green Tea, Rwandan Rukeri Black Tea

OTHER FRUITS Fancy Formosa Oolong Tea, Yunnan Golden Tips Black Tea

PORK Goddess of Mercy Oolong Tea, Irish Breakfast Tea, Tippy Yunnan Black Tea

TROPICAL FRUITS Jade Oolong Tea, Luan Guapian Green Tea, Oriental Beauty Oolong Tea

VANILLA/PLAIN Cream Earl Grey Black Tea, Taiwanese Gui Fei Oolong Tea, fruity tisanes

VEGETABLES Winey Keemun Black Tea, Genmaicha Green Tea, Gaba Oolong Tea

It is always a good idea to prepare the chosen tea in advance of the event to verify that the pairing is pleasing and to determine the most beneficial water temperature (not all tea requires boiling water) and steep time. For a list of purveyors of fine teas such as these, turn to page 132.

CLASSIC
CREAM SCONES,
page 15

PLAIN
Scones

TRADITIONAL AND PURE SCONES, FROM CLASSIC
CREAM TO DELICIOUS VANILLA-BUTTERMILK,
ARE ALWAYS SUITABLE AND TIME-HONORED
CHOICES FOR AFTERNOON TEA.

Classic Cream Scones
Makes 10

This timeless scone is marvelous year-round, in any season, and for any occasion. It's the epitome of classic with its traditional shape and beloved taste. You can never go wrong with serving cream scones for afternoon tea!

2½ cups all-purpose flour
¼ cup granulated sugar
2½ teaspoons baking powder
½ teaspoon fine sea salt
¼ cup unsalted butter, frozen
¾ cup plus 1 tablespoon cold heavy whipping cream, divided
2 large eggs, divided
½ teaspoon vanilla extract

• Preheat oven to 350°. Line a rimmed baking sheet with parchment paper.
• In a large bowl, whisk together flour, sugar, baking powder, and salt. Using a coarse grater, grate frozen butter into flour mixture. Stir until grated butter is coated and evenly distributed.
• In a medium bowl, whisk together ¾ cup cream, 1 egg, and vanilla extract. Add to flour mixture, stirring until a shaggy dough begins to form. Working gently, bring mixture together in bowl with hands until a dough forms. (If dough won't come together, add more cream, 1 table-spoon at a time, until it does. Dough should be firm.)
• Turn out dough onto a lightly floured surface, and knead gently until smooth by patting dough and folding it in half 4 to 5 times. Using a rolling pin, roll out dough to a ¾-inch thickness. Using a 2½-inch fluted round cutter dipped in flour, cut 10 scones from dough with-out twisting cutter, rerolling scraps as necessary. Place scones 2 inches apart on prepared baking sheet.
• In a small bowl, whisk together remaining 1 table-spoon cream and remaining 1 egg to make an egg wash. Brush tops of scones with egg wash.
• Bake until edges of scones are golden brown and a wooden pick inserted in the centers comes out clean, approximately 20 minutes. Serve warm.

RECOMMENDED CONDIMENTS:
Clotted cream | Black currant curd

Cream Scones

Makes 12 to 14

Quintessential for afternoon tea, these traditional and tender scones never disappoint and always provide the ideal vehicle for condiment consumption. This recipe utilizes cake flour instead of all-purpose flour to give these scones a soft, smooth texture.

2 cups cake flour
2 tablespoons granulated sugar
2½ teaspoons baking powder
½ teaspoon fine sea salt
4 tablespoons cold salted butter, cubed
¾ cup plus 3 tablespoons cold heavy whipping cream, divided

• Preheat oven to 400°. Line a rimmed baking sheet with parchment paper.
• In a large bowl, whisk together flour, sugar, baking powder, and salt. Using a pastry blender or 2 forks, cut butter into flour mixture until it resembles coarse crumbs.
• Add ¾ cup plus 2 tablespoons cream to flour mixture, stirring until a shaggy dough begins to form. Working gently, bring mixture together in bowl with hands until a dough forms. (If dough won't come together, add more cream, 1 tablespoon at a time, until it does. Dough should be very firm.)
• Turn out dough onto a lightly floured surface, and knead gently by patting dough and folding it in half 3 to 4 times. Using a rolling pin, roll out dough to a ½-inch thickness. Using a 2-inch fluted round cutter dipped in flour, cut as many scones as possible from dough without twisting cutter, rerolling scraps as necessary. Place scones 2 inches apart on prepared baking sheet.
• Brush tops of scones with remaining 1 tablespoon cream.
• Bake until edges of scones are light golden brown and a wooden pick inserted in the centers comes out clean, approximately 10 minutes. Serve warm.

RECOMMENDED CONDIMENTS:
Clotted cream | Lemon curd

European Butter Scones
Makes 8

With European-style butter worked into the dough, one bite of this scrumptious scone will instantly transport you abroad to your favorite tearoom.

1½ cups all-purpose flour
1 cup pastry flour
¼ cup granulated sugar
1 teaspoon baking powder
½ teaspoon fine sea salt
6 tablespoons cold European-style unsalted butter*, cubed
½ cup plus 1 tablespoon cold heavy whipping cream, divided
1 large egg
½ teaspoon vanilla extract

• Preheat oven to 350°. Line a rimmed baking sheet with parchment paper.
• In a large bowl, whisk together all-purpose flour, pastry flour, sugar, baking powder, and salt. Using a pastry blender or 2 forks, cut in butter until it resembles coarse crumbs.
• In a small bowl, whisk together ½ cup cream, egg, and vanilla extract. Add to flour mixture, stirring until a shaggy dough begins to form. Working gently, bring mixture together in bowl with hands until a dough forms. (If dough won't come together, add more cream, 1 tablespoon at a time, until it does. Dough should be firm.)
• Turn out dough onto a lightly floured surface, and knead gently until smooth by patting dough and folding it in half 4 to 5 times. Using a rolling pin, roll out dough to a 1-inch thickness. Using a 2¼-inch fluted round cutter dipped in flour, cut 8 scones from dough without

twisting cutter, rerolling scraps as necessary. Place scones 2 inches apart on prepared baking sheet.
• Brush top of scones with remaining 1 tablespoon cream.
• Bake until edges of scones are golden brown and a wooden pick inserted in the centers comes out clean, approximately 20 minutes. Serve warm.

European-style butter has more butterfat than regular butter does. We used Plugrá European Style Unsalted Butter.

RECOMMENDED CONDIMENTS:
Vanilla–Crème Fraîche Cream (recipe on page 124) | Strawberry jam

Challah Scones
Makes 12

In our tea-sized take on traditional Jewish fare, we incorporate the familiar flavors of challah bread—enriched by eggs and topped with sesame seeds—but simplify the baking process by cutting down the steps and rise time. These tasty scones are easy to prepare and best when served warm from the oven.

2 cups all-purpose flour
¼ cup granulated sugar
2 teaspoons baking powder
½ teaspoon fine sea salt
4 tablespoons cold salted butter, cubed
¾ cup cold heavy whipping cream
2 large egg yolks
1 large egg
1 teaspoon sesame seed

• Preheat oven to 350°. Line a rimmed baking sheet with parchment paper.
• In a large bowl, whisk together flour, sugar, baking powder, and salt. Using a pastry blender or 2 forks, cut butter into flour mixture until it resembles coarse crumbs.
• In a small bowl, whisk together cream and egg yolks. Add to flour mixture, stirring until a shaggy dough begins to form. Working gently, bring mixture together in bowl with hands until a dough forms. (If dough won't come together, add more cream, 1 tablespoon at a time, until it does. Dough should be firm.)

• Turn out dough onto a lightly floured surface, and knead gently until smooth by patting dough and folding it in half 4 to 5 times. Using a rolling pin, roll out dough to a ¾-inch thickness. Using a 2-inch fluted round cutter dipped in flour, cut 12 scones from dough without twisting cutter, rerolling scraps as necessary. Place scones 2 inches apart on prepared baking sheet.
• In a small bowl, whisk egg. Brush tops of scones with egg, and sprinkle with sesame seed.
• Bake until edges of scones are golden brown and a wooden pick inserted in the centers comes out clean, 14 to 15 minutes. Serve warm.

RECOMMENDED CONDIMENTS:
Clotted cream | Currant jam | Lemon curd

• Add cold vanilla-infused cream to flour mixture, stirring until a shaggy dough begins to form. Working gently, bring mixture together in bowl with hands until a dough forms. (If dough won't come together, add more cream, 1 tablespoon at a time, until it does. Dough should be firm.)
• Turn out dough onto a lightly floured surface, and knead gently by patting dough and folding it in half 3 times. Using a rolling pin, roll out dough to a ½-inch thickness. Using a 2-inch fluted round cutter dipped in flour, cut 18 scones from dough without twisting cutter, rerolling scraps as necessary. Place scones 2 inches apart on prepared baking sheet.
• Sprinkle tops of scones evenly with vanilla sugar.
• Bake until edges of scones are light golden brown and a wooden pick inserted in the centers comes out clean, approximately 20 minutes. Serve warm.

We used Penzeys.

RECOMMENDED CONDIMENTS:
Faux Clotted Cream (recipe on page 122) | *Spiced Pear Compote (recipe on page 127)*

Vanilla Bean Scones
Makes 18

Delicate and creamy, these gentle and mouthwatering morsels always satisfy when it comes to teatime.

¾ cup plus 2 tablespoons heavy whipping cream
1 vanilla bean, split, scraped, and seeds reserved
2 cups all-purpose flour
⅓ cup granulated sugar
2 teaspoons baking powder
½ teaspoon fine sea salt
5 tablespoons salted butter, cubed
1 tablespoon vanilla sugar*

• In a small saucepan, heat together cream and reserved vanilla bean seeds just to a simmer. Remove from heat, and pour into a covered container. Refrigerate until very cold, at least 8 hours or overnight.
• Preheat oven to 350°. Line a rimmed baking sheet with parchment paper.
• In a large bowl, whisk together flour, granulated sugar, baking powder, and salt. Using a pastry blender or 2 forks, cut butter into flour mixture until it resembles coarse crumbs.

Vanilla-Buttermilk Scones
Makes 12

While bold, flavorful scones can be a welcome commencement for afternoon tea, there is beauty in a simple pastry— like these subtly imparted with vanilla and buttermilk— especially when served with clotted cream and a pair of flavorful jams.

2½ cups all-purpose flour
⅓ cup granulated sugar
2½ teaspoons baking powder
½ teaspoon fine sea salt
4 tablespoons cold unsalted butter, cubed
⅔ cup plus 1 tablespoon buttermilk, divided
1 large egg, lightly beaten
1 tablespoon vanilla bean paste

• Preheat oven to 375°. Line a rimmed baking sheet with parchment paper.
• In a large bowl, whisk together flour, sugar, baking powder, and salt. Using a pastry blender or 2 forks, cut butter into flour mixture until it resembles coarse crumbs.
• In a medium bowl, whisk together ⅔ cup buttermilk,

egg, and vanilla bean paste. Add to flour mixture, stirring until a shaggy dough begins to form. Working gently, bring mixture together in bowl with hands until a dough forms. (If dough won't come together, add more buttermilk, 1 tablespoon at a time, until it does. Dough should be firm.)

• Turn out dough onto a lightly floured surface, and knead gently until smooth by patting dough and folding it in half 3 to 4 times. Using a rolling pin, roll out dough to a 1-inch thickness. Using a floured 2-inch round cutter dipped in flour, cut 12 scones from dough without twisting cutter, rerolling scraps as necessary. Place scones, evenly spaced, on prepared baking sheet.

• Brush tops of scones with remaining 1 tablespoon buttermilk.

• Bake until scones are lightly browned, 13 to 15 minutes. Remove from oven and let cool on pan for 10 minutes. Serve warm.

RECOMMENDED CONDIMENTS:

Clotted cream | Blueberry preserves | Rose petal confit*

*We used Favols Les Créatives Confit Pétales de Roses, available on amazon.com.

Angel Scones
Makes approximately 24

These heavenly, wedge-shaped delights will become your go-to recipe for all sorts of teatime gatherings. Fluffy and truly mouthwatering, these scones are a variation on the Southern angel biscuit and get their "lift" from yeast and baking powder.

1 teaspoon active-dry yeast
¼ cup warm (110°) water
2 cups all-purpose flour
¼ cup granulated sugar
½ teaspoon fine sea salt
¼ teaspoon baking powder
4 tablespoons cold salted butter, cubed
½ cup plus 2 tablespoons cold heavy whipping cream

• Lightly coat a rimmed baking sheet with a neutral oil.
• In a small bowl, dissolve yeast in warm water. Let stand for 5 minutes.
• In a large bowl, whisk together flour, sugar, salt, and baking powder. Using a pastry blender or 2 forks, cut butter into flour mixture until it resembles coarse crumbs.

• In a liquid-measuring cup, whisk together yeast mixture and cream. Add to flour mixture, stirring until a shaggy dough begins to form. Working gently, bring mixture together in bowl with hands until a dough forms. (If dough won't come together, add more cream, 1 tablespoon at a time, until it does. Dough should be somewhat firm.)
• Turn dough out onto a lightly floured surface, and knead approximately 12 times, folding and turning dough in quarter turns. Using a rolling pin, roll out dough to a ½-inch thickness. Using a 2-inch triangle-shaped cutter dipped in flour, cut as many scones as possible from dough without twisting cutter. Place scones 2 inches apart on prepared baking sheet. Cover with a thin dish towel.
• Place a pan of very hot (boiling) water on bottom rack of an unheated oven. Place baking sheet with covered scones on rack above pan. Let scones rise in oven with door closed for 1 hour. Remove scones and pan of water from oven.
• Preheat oven to 425°.
• Bake scones until golden brown, approximately 8 minutes. Serve warm.

RECOMMENDED CONDIMENT:
Spiced Cream (recipe on page 123)

Almond–Cream Cheese Scones
Makes 19

Imparted with nutty notes from ground and chopped almonds and splendid richness from cream cheese, these terrific and well-rounded scones are texturally divine.

2 cups all-purpose flour
½ cup ground toasted almonds
¼ cup granulated sugar
2½ teaspoons baking powder
½ teaspoon fine sea salt
4 tablespoons cold salted butter, cubed
1 (3-ounce) package cream cheese, cubed
¼ cup chopped toasted almonds
¾ cup plus 1 tablespoon cold heavy whipping cream, divided
¼ teaspoon vanilla extract
¼ teaspoon almond extract

- Preheat oven to 350°. Line a rimmed baking sheet with parchment paper.
- In a medium bowl, whisk together flour, ground almonds, sugar, baking powder, and salt. Using a pastry blender or 2 forks, cut butter into flour mixture until it resembles coarse crumbs. Stir in cream cheese and chopped almonds.
- In a liquid-measuring cup, stir together ¾ cup cream, vanilla extract, and almond extract. Add to flour mixture, stirring until a shaggy dough begins to form. Working gently, bring mixture together in bowl with hands until a dough forms. (If dough won't come together, add more cream, 1 tablespoon at a time, until it does. Dough should be somewhat firm.)
- Turn out dough onto a lightly floured surface, and knead gently until smooth by patting dough and folding it in half 4 to 5 times. Using a rolling pin, roll out dough to a ½-inch thickness. Using a 2½-inch triangle-shaped cutter dipped in flour, cut 19 scones from dough, rerolling scraps as necessary. Place scones 2 inches apart on prepared baking sheet.
- Brush tops of scones with remaining 1 table-spoon cream.
- Bake until edges are golden brown, approximately 20 minutes. Serve warm.

RECOMMENDED CONDIMENT:
Honeyed Crème Fraîche (recipe on page 124)

Browned Butter–Vanilla Scones
Makes 9

Browning the butter in this recipe adds a dynamic depth of flavor and slightly nutty aroma, which is perfectly balanced by the addition of vanilla bean seeds.

1 vanilla bean pod
8 tablespoons unsalted butter, cubed
2½ cups all-purpose flour
⅓ cup granulated sugar
1 tablespoon baking powder
½ teaspoon fine sea salt
1 cup plus 1 tablespoon cold heavy whipping cream, divided
½ teaspoon vanilla extract

• Using a sharp knife, split vanilla bean pod lengthwise, and scrape seeds.
• In a small saucepan, melt butter over medium heat. Add vanilla bean seeds and scraped pod. Cook, stirring occasionally, until butter turns golden brown and has a nutty aroma. Remove vanilla bean pod. Pour browned butter into a heatproof bowl and let cool. Cover and refrigerate until solid, up to a day in advance.
• Preheat oven to 350°. Line a rimmed baking sheet with parchment paper.
• In a large bowl, whisk together flour, sugar, baking powder, and salt. Using a pastry blender or 2 forks, cut in cold browned butter until it resembles coarse crumbs.
• In a small bowl, stir together 1 cup cream and vanilla extract. Add cream mixture to flour mixture, stirring until a shaggy dough begins to form. Working gently, bring mixture together in bowl with hands until a dough forms. (If dough won't come together, add more cream, 1 tablespoon at a time, until it does. Dough should be firm.)
• Turn out dough onto a lightly floured surface, and knead gently by patting dough and folding it in half 4 to 5 times. Using a rolling pin, roll out dough to a 1-inch thickness. Using a 2¼-inch fluted round cutter dipped in flour, cut 9 scones from dough without twisting cutter, rerolling scraps as necessary. Place scones 2 inches apart on prepared baking sheet.
• Brush tops of scones with remaining 1 tablespoon cream.

• Bake until edges of scones are golden brown and a wooden pick inserted in the centers comes out clean, 20 to 21 minutes. Serve warm.

RECOMMENDED CONDIMENTS:
Clotted cream | Black currant curd

Brown Sugar–Cream Cheese Scones
Makes 12

Bits of cream cheese add luscious texture to these delightful bakes, which are sweetened solely with brown sugar. Created as an homage to the flavors of the iconic Mardi Gras pastry, King Cake, these teatime treats are perfect then as well as anytime of the year.

2 cups all-purpose flour
1/3 cup firmly packed light brown sugar
2 teaspoons baking powder
1/2 teaspoon fine sea salt
4 tablespoons cold salted butter, cubed
3 ounces cream cheese, cubed
3/4 cup plus 2 tablespoons cold heavy whipping
    cream, divided
1/2 teaspoon vanilla extract
Garnish: turbinado sugar

• Preheat oven to 350°. Line a rimmed baking sheet with parchment paper.
• In a large bowl, whisk together flour, brown sugar, baking powder, and salt. Using a pastry blender or 2 forks, cut butter into flour mixture until it resembles coarse crumbs. Gently stir in cream cheese, leaving cubes intact.
• In a small bowl, stir together 3/4 cup plus 1 table-spoon cream and vanilla extract. Add to flour mixture, stirring gently until a shaggy dough begins to form. Working gently, bring mixture together in bowl with hands until a dough forms. (If dough won't come together, add more cream, 1 tablespoon at a time, until it does. Dough should be somewhat firm.)

• Turn out dough onto a lightly floured surface, and knead gently until smooth by patting dough and folding it in half 4 to 5 times. Using a rolling pin, roll out dough to a 3/4-inch thickness. Using a 2¼-inch fluted round cutter dipped in flour, cut 12 scones from dough without twisting cutter, rerolling scraps as necessary. Place scones 2 inches apart on prepared baking sheet.
• Brush tops of scones with remaining 1 tablespoon cream. Garnish tops of scones with turbinado sugar, if desired.
• Bake until edges of scones are golden brown and a wooden pick inserted in the centers comes out clean, approximately 20 minutes. Serve warm.

RECOMMENDED CONDIMENTS:
Clotted cream | Strawberry jam

STRAWBERRY, LAVENDER &
WHITE CHOCOLATE SCONES,
page 49

SWEET

Scones

FLAVORED BY FRUITS, NUTS, CHOCOLATE,
SPICES, AND MORE, THESE DELECTABLE AND
DECADENT TREATS ARE SURE TO PLEASE,
ESPECIALLY WHEN PAIRED WITH TEA.

Sultana-Buttermilk Scones

Makes 12

Tangy buttermilk is the perfect ingredient to balance out the subtle sweetness of chewy golden raisins (also known as sultanas) in this classic and tasty treat.

3 cups all-purpose flour
⅓ cup granulated sugar
4 teaspoons baking powder
½ teaspoon fine sea salt
8 tablespoons cold unsalted butter, cubed
½ cup sultanas (golden raisins)
2 large eggs, lightly beaten, divided
¾ cup cold whole buttermilk

• Line a rimmed baking sheet with parchment paper.
• In a large bowl, whisk together flour, sugar, baking powder, and salt. Using a pastry blender or 2 forks, cut butter into flour mixture until it resembles coarse crumbs. Stir in sultanas.
• Using a fork, stir 1 egg into flour mixture just until combined. Stir in buttermilk just until dry ingredients are moistened. Working gently, bring mixture together in bowl with hands until a dough forms. Gently knead 3 to 4 times.
• Turn out dough onto a lightly floured surface. Cover dough and let rest at room temperature for 10 minutes.
• Using a rolling pin, roll out dough to a 1-inch thickness. Using a 2¼-inch fluted round cutter dipped in flour, cut 12 scones from dough without twisting cutter, rerolling scraps as necessary. Place scones 1 inch apart on prepared baking sheet. Let stand at room temperature for 30 minutes.
• Meanwhile, preheat oven to 375°.
• Brush tops of scones with remaining 1 egg.
• Bake until tops of scones are golden brown and a wooden pick inserted in the centers comes out clean, 15 to 20 minutes. Serve warm.

RECOMMENDED CONDIMENTS:
Clotted cream | Orange marmalade

Golden Raisin Scones

Makes 16

This traditional and familiar scone flavor boasts a delicious upgrade with our tasty Confectioners' Sugar Glaze atop the bake.

2¼ cups all-purpose flour
¼ cup granulated sugar
2¼ teaspoons baking powder
½ teaspoon ground mace
½ teaspoon fine sea salt
5 tablespoons cold salted butter, cubed
½ cup golden raisins
¾ cup plus 1 tablespoon cold heavy whipping cream
1 large egg
½ teaspoon vanilla extract
Confectioners' Sugar Glaze (recipe follows)

• Preheat oven to 350°. Line 2 baking sheets with parchment paper.
• In a large bowl, whisk together flour, sugar, baking powder, mace, and salt. Using a pastry blender or 2 forks, cut butter into flour mixture until it resembles coarse crumbs. Stir in raisins until coated with flour.
• In a small bowl, whisk together cream, egg, and vanilla extract. Add to flour mixture, stirring until a shaggy dough begins to form. Working gently, bring mixture together in bowl with hands until a dough forms. (If dough won't come together, add more cream, 1 table-spoon at a time, until it does. Dough should be firm.)
• Turn out dough onto a lightly floured surface, and knead gently until smooth by patting dough and folding it in half 3 to 4 times. Using a rolling pin, roll out dough to a ½-inch thickness. Using a 2½-inch round cutter dipped in flour, cut 16 scones from dough without twist-ing cutter, rerolling scraps as necessary. Place scones 2 inches apart on prepared baking sheets.
• Bake until edges of scones are light golden brown and a wooden pick inserted in the centers comes out clean, approximately 15 minutes. Transfer scones to a wire rack, and let cool completely.
• When cool, spoon Confectioners' Sugar Glaze over tops of scones, and let dry.

RECOMMENDED CONDIMENT:
Orange marmalade

Confectioners' Sugar Glaze

Makes ⅓ cup

This smooth glaze will appear as if it's barely there when spooned over our Golden Raisin Scones; however, the taste will be satisfyingly noticeable.

¾ cup confectioners' sugar
2 tablespoons whole milk

• In a small bowl, whisk together confectioners' sugar and milk until smooth and creamy. Use immediately.

Golden Raisin–Tarragon Scones
Makes 9

Studded with golden raisins and flavorful fresh tarragon, these terrific scones are a summertime delight and are even prettier when garnished with your favorite berries and edible flowers.

2 cups all-purpose flour
¼ cup granulated sugar
2 teaspoons baking powder
½ teaspoon fine sea salt
4 tablespoons cold unsalted butter, cubed
⅓ cup golden raisins
1 teaspoon finely chopped fresh tarragon
¾ cup plus 3 tablespoons cold heavy cream, divided
¼ teaspoon vanilla extract
Garnish: blueberries, blackberries, fresh tarragon,
    and fresh edible flowers*

• Preheat oven to 350°. Line a rimmed baking sheet with parchment paper.
• In a large bowl, whisk together flour, sugar, baking powder, and salt. Using a pastry blender or 2 forks, cut butter into flour mixture until it resembles coarse crumbs. Stir in raisins and tarragon.
• In a small bowl, stir together ¾ cup plus 2 tablespoons cream and vanilla extract. Add to flour mixture, stirring until a shaggy dough begins to form. Working gently, bring mixture together in bowl with hands until a dough forms. (If dough won't come together, add more cream, 1 tablespoon at a time, until it does. Dough should be firm.)
• Turn out dough onto a lightly floured surface, and knead gently by patting dough and folding it in half 5 to 7 times. Using a rolling pin, roll out dough to a 1-inch thickness. Using a 2¼-inch fluted round cutter dipped in flour, cut 9 scones from dough without twisting cutter, rerolling scraps as necessary. Place scones 2 inches apart on prepared baking sheet.
• Brush tops of scones with remaining 1 tablespoon cream.
• Bake until edges of scones are golden brown and a wooden pick inserted in the centers comes out clean, approximately 20 minutes.

Edible flowers are available from Gourmet Sweet Botanicals, 800-931-7530, gourmetsweetbotanicals.com.

RECOMMENDED CONDIMENTS:
Clotted cream | Lemon curd

Cranberry-Basil Scones
Makes 10

Scones flavored by tart cranberries and fresh basil are made even tastier when a delectable layer of sugar and lemon juice is spooned on top.

2 cups all-purpose flour
2 tablespoons granulated sugar
2 teaspoons baking powder
2 teaspoons fresh lemon zest
½ teaspoon fine sea salt
4 tablespoons cold salted butter, cubed
½ cup dried cranberries
3 tablespoons chopped fresh basil
¾ cup cold heavy whipping cream
½ cup plus 2 tablespoons confectioners' sugar
2 tablespoons fresh lemon juice

• Preheat oven to 350°. Line a rimmed baking sheet with parchment paper.
• In a large bowl, whisk together flour, granulated sugar, baking powder, lemon zest, and salt. Using a pastry blender or 2 forks, cut butter into flour mixture until it resembles coarse crumbs. Stir in cranberries and basil.
• Add cream to flour mixture, stirring until a shaggy dough begins to form. Working gently, bring mixture together in bowl with hands until a dough forms. (If dough won't come together, add more cream, 1 table-spoon at a time, until it does. Dough should be firm.)
• Turn out dough onto a lightly floured surface, and knead gently until smooth by patting dough and folding it in half 3 to 5 times. Using a rolling pin, roll out dough to a ¾-inch thickness. Using a 2-inch square cutter dipped in flour, cut 10 scones from dough without twist-ing cutter, rerolling scraps as necessary. Place scones 2 inches apart on prepared baking sheet.
• Bake until edges of scones are golden brown and a wooden pick inserted in the centers comes out clean, 18 to 20 minutes. Let cool on a wire rack set over a rimmed baking sheet.
• In a small bowl, whisk together confectioners' sugar and lemon juice until smooth. Spoon over cooled scones on wire cooling rack and let dry before serving.

RECOMMENDED CONDIMENTS:
Clotted cream | Lemon curd

Cranberry-Orange Scones

Makes 9

The fruity and bright flavors of dried cranberries and fresh orange zest are beautifully balanced in this fantastic scone.

2 cups all-purpose flour
½ cup granulated sugar
1 tablespoon baking powder
1 tablespoon fresh orange zest
¼ teaspoon fine sea salt
8 tablespoons cold salted butter, cubed
½ cup dried cranberries
6 tablespoons cold whole milk
2 large eggs, beaten and divided
1 teaspoon turbinado sugar

• Preheat oven to 425°. Line a rimmed baking sheet with parchment paper.
• In a large bowl, whisk together flour, granulated sugar, baking powder, orange zest, and salt. Using a pastry blender or 2 forks, cut butter into flour mixture until it resembles coarse crumbs. Stir in cranberries.

• In a small bowl, whisk together milk and 1 egg. Add to flour mixture, stirring until a shaggy dough begins to form. Working gently, bring mixture together in bowl with hands until a dough forms. (If dough won't come together, add more milk, 1 tablespoon at a time, until it does. Dough should be firm.)
• Turn out dough onto a lightly floured surface, and knead gently until smooth by patting dough and folding it in half 6 to 8 times. Using a rolling pin, roll out dough to a ¾-inch thickness. Using a 2½-inch round cutter dipped in flour, cut 9 scones from dough without twisting cutter, rerolling scraps as necessary. Place scones 2 inches apart on prepared baking sheet.
• Brush tops of scones with remaining beaten egg, and sprinkle with turbinado sugar.
• Bake until edges of scones are golden brown and a wooden pick inserted in centers comes out clean, 10 to 12 minutes.

RECOMMENDED CONDIMENTS:
Vanilla Cream (recipe on page 122) | Lemon Curd (recipe on page 128)

Rosemary-Lemon Scones
Makes 12

Brilliantly crowned with lemon zest curls and fresh rose-mary sprigs, these vibrant and herb-laced scones are a gift to the palate and look splendid when served on a tiered stand. Lemonade is the secret ingredient to making these scrumptious scones, which are filled with bright flavor in every bite.

1½ cups all-purpose flour
½ cup cake flour
2 tablespoons granulated sugar
2 teaspoons fresh lemon zest
1 teaspoon baking powder
½ teaspoon baking soda
½ teaspoon fine sea salt
5 tablespoons cold unsalted butter, cubed
½ cup cold whole milk
¼ cup cold lemonade
1 large egg, beaten
¼ cup turbinado sugar
Garnish: fresh lemon zest curls, fresh rosemary sprigs

• Preheat oven to 375°. Line a rimmed baking sheet with parchment paper.
• In a large bowl, whisk together all-purpose flour, cake flour, granulated sugar, lemon zest, baking powder, baking soda, and salt. Using a pastry blender or 2 forks, cut in butter until it resembles coarse crumbs.
• In a small bowl, stir together milk and lemonade. Add milk mixture to flour mixture, stirring until a shaggy dough begins to form. Working gently, bring mixture together in bowl with hands until a dough forms. (If dough won't come together, add more milk, 1 table-spoon at a time, until it does. Dough should be firm.)
• Turn out dough onto a lightly floured surface, and knead gently until smooth by patting dough and folding it in half 4 to 5 times. Using a rolling pin, roll out dough to a ½-inch thickness. Using a 2-inch fluted round cutter dipped in flour, cut 12 scones from dough without twisting cutter, rerolling scraps as necessary. Place scones 2 inches apart on prepared baking sheet.
• Brush tops of scones with egg, and sprinkle with turbinado sugar.

• Bake until edges of scones are golden brown and a wooden pick inserted in centers comes out clean, 12 to 15 minutes.
• Garnish with lemon zest curls and rosemary sprigs, if desired.

RECOMMENDED CONDIMENTS:
Clotted cream | Lemon Curd (recipe on page 128)

Mixed Berry & Thyme Scones
Makes 18

A medley of dried berries—including cranberries, raisins, and blueberries—pairs delightfully with the herbaceous flavor of fresh thyme in these sweet scones.

2½ cups all-purpose flour
⅓ cup plus 1 teaspoon granulated sugar, divided
1 tablespoon baking powder
1 teaspoon finely chopped fresh thyme
½ teaspoon fine sea salt
4 tablespoons cold unsalted butter, cubed
¾ cup dried mixed berries*
½ cup plus 4 tablespoons cold heavy whipping cream, divided
1 large egg
½ teaspoon vanilla extract

• Preheat oven to 375°. Line a rimmed baking sheet with parchment paper.
• In a large bowl, whisk together flour, ⅓ cup granulated sugar, baking powder, thyme, and salt. Using a pastry blender or 2 forks, cut butter into flour mixture until it resembles coarse crumbs. Stir in dried berries.
• In a small bowl, whisk together ½ cup plus 3 table-spoons cream, egg, and vanilla extract. Add to flour mixture, stirring until a shaggy dough begins to form. Working gently, bring mixture together in bowl with hands until a dough forms. (If dough won't come together, add more cream, 1 tablespoon at a time, until it does. Dough should be firm.)
• Turn out dough onto a lightly floured surface, and knead gently until smooth by patting dough and folding it in half 4 to 5 times. Using a rolling pin, roll out dough to a ¾-inch thickness. Using a 2-inch fluted round cut-ter dipped in flour, cut 18 scones from dough without twisting cutter, rerolling scraps as necessary. Place scones, evenly spaced, on prepared baking sheet.
• Brush tops of scones lightly with remaining 1 tablespoon cream and sprinkle with remaining 1 teaspoon sugar.
• Bake until edges of scones are golden brown and a wooden pick inserted in the centers comes out clean, 18 to 20 minutes. Serve warm.

We used Publix GreenWise Dried Berry Blend.

RECOMMENDED CONDIMENTS:
Clotted cream | Lemon Curd (recipe on page 128)

Banoffee Scones
Makes 12

Inspired by a traditional British dessert, these Banoffee Scones include ripe bananas and milk chocolate toffee bits. Top them with clotted cream to really make these scones over-the-top scrumptious.

2 cups all-purpose flour
½ cup bread flour
½ cup caster sugar
1 tablespoon baking powder
¼ teaspoon fine sea salt
5 tablespoons cold unsalted butter, cubed
½ cup milk chocolate toffee bits
6 tablespoons mashed ripe banana
2 large eggs, divided
2 tablespoons whole buttermilk, divided

• Preheat oven to 375°. Line a rimmed baking sheet with parchment paper.
• In a large bowl, whisk together all-purpose flour, bread flour, sugar, baking powder, and salt. Using a pastry blender or 2 forks, cut butter into flour mixture until it resembles coarse crumbs. Stir in toffee bits.

• In a small bowl, whisk together banana, 1 egg, and 1 tablespoon buttermilk. Add to flour mixture, stirring until a shaggy dough begins to form. Working gently, bring mixture together in bowl with hands until a dough forms. (If dough won't come together, add more buttermilk, 1 tablespoon at a time, until it does. Dough should be firm.)
• Turn out dough onto a lightly floured surface, and knead gently until smooth by patting dough and folding it in half 3 to 4 times. Using a rolling pin, roll out dough to a ½-inch thickness. Using a 2¼-inch round cutter dipped in flour, cut 12 scones from dough without twisting cutter, rerolling scraps as necessary. Place on prepared baking sheet. Freeze for 10 minutes.
• In a small bowl, whisk together remaining 1 egg and remaining 1 tablespoon buttermilk to make an egg wash. Brush tops of scones with egg wash.
• Bake until scones are golden brown and a wooden pick inserted in the centers comes out clean, approximately 14 minutes. Serve warm.

RECOMMENDED CONDIMENT:
Clotted cream

Pineapple Scones
Makes 14

This toothsome scone, with lots of sweet, dried pineapple, is a wonderful treat for a summertime tea, and the whimsical flower shape adds visual interest.

2 cups all-purpose flour
⅓ cup plus 1 teaspoon granulated sugar, divided
2 teaspoons baking powder
½ teaspoon fine sea salt
4 tablespoons cold salted butter, cubed
1 cup chopped sweetened dried pineapple*
¾ cup plus 2 tablespoons cold heavy whipping cream, divided
½ teaspoon vanilla extract

• Preheat oven to 350°. Line a rimmed baking sheet with parchment paper.
• In a large bowl, whisk together flour, ⅓ cup sugar, baking powder, and salt. Using a pastry blender or 2 forks, cut butter into flour mixture until it resembles coarse crumbs. Stir in pineapple.

• In a small bowl, stir together ¾ cup plus 1 tablespoon cream and vanilla extract. Add to flour mixture, stirring until a shaggy dough begins to form. Working gently, bring mixture together in bowl with hands until a dough forms. (If dough won't come together, add more cream, 1 tablespoon at a time, until it does. Dough should be firm.)
• Turn out dough onto a lightly floured surface, and knead gently by patting dough and folding it in half 4 to 5 times. Using a rolling pin, roll out dough to a ¾-inch thickness. Using a 2¼-inch flower-shaped cutter dipped in flour, cut 14 scones from dough without twisting cutter, rerolling scraps as necessary. Place scones 2 inches apart on prepared baking sheet.
• Brush tops of scones with remaining 1 tablespoon cream, and sprinkle with remaining 1 teaspoon sugar.
• Bake until edges of scones are golden brown and a wooden pick inserted in the centers comes out clean, approximately 20 minutes. Serve warm.

We used 365 Everyday Value Sweetened Dried Pineapple, available at Whole Foods Market.

RECOMMENDED CONDIMENTS:
Clotted cream | Lemon curd

Papaya-Lime Scones
Makes 11

The bright flavors of dried papaya and fresh lime zest inter-mingle in this delightful scone, and a drizzle of Lime Glaze adds the perfect amount of sweetness and zing.

2 cups all-purpose flour
⅓ cup granulated sugar
2 teaspoons baking powder
2 teaspoons fresh lime zest
½ teaspoon fine sea salt
4 tablespoons cold salted butter, cubed
¾ cup chopped dried papaya, divided
1 cup cold heavy whipping cream
½ teaspoon vanilla extract
Lime Glaze (recipe follows)

• Preheat oven to 350°. Line a rimmed baking sheet with parchment paper.
• In a large bowl, whisk together flour, sugar, baking powder, lime zest, and salt. Using a pastry blender or 2 forks, cut butter into flour mixture until it resembles coarse crumbs. Stir in papaya, reserving 2 tablespoons papaya for scone centers.
• In a liquid-measuring cup, stir together cream and vanilla extract. Add to flour mixture, stirring until a shaggy dough begins to form. Working gently, bring mixture together in bowl with hands until a dough forms. (If dough won't come together, add more cream, 1 tablespoon at a time, until it does. Dough should be firm.)
• Turn out dough onto a lightly floured surface, and knead gently by patting dough and folding it in half 4 to 5 times. Using a rolling pin, roll out dough to a ½-inch thickness. Using a 2½-inch flower-shaped cutter dipped in flour, cut 11 scones from dough without twisting cut-ter, rerolling scraps as necessary. Place scones 2 inches apart on prepared baking sheet. Using thumb or the rounded back of a measuring spoon, press an indenta-tion into centers of scones.
• Bake until edges of scones are golden brown and a wooden pick inserted in the centers comes out clean, approximately 20 minutes. Let cool completely on a wire rack set over a rimmed baking sheet.
• Spoon Lime Glaze over scones. Divide reserved chopped papaya among centers of scones. Let glaze dry on scones before serving, approximately 1 hour.

RECOMMENDED CONDIMENTS:
Clotted cream | Lemon curd

Lime Glaze
Makes 1 cup

Freshly squeezed lime juice is the secret to this tangy topping.

2 cups confectioners' sugar
¼ cup plus 2 tablespoons fresh lime juice

• In a medium bowl, whisk together confectioners' sugar and lime juice until smooth. Use immediately.

Lemon-Coconut Scones
Makes 12

Laced with fresh lemon zest and toasted coconut, these plump confections are also made with coconut milk. Serve them at a tea party in warm weather or whenever a taste of the tropics is needed.

¾ cup sweetened flaked coconut
3 cups all-purpose flour
½ cup granulated sugar
1½ tablespoons fresh lemon zest
1 tablespoon baking powder
¾ teaspoon fine sea salt
8 tablespoons cold unsalted butter, cubed
¾ cup plus 2 tablespoons unsweetened coconut milk, divided
½ teaspoon vanilla extract

• Preheat oven to 400°. Line 2 rimmed baking sheets with parchment paper.
• On a prepared baking sheet, spread coconut in an even layer.
• Bake coconut for 2 minutes. Stir coconut and return to oven. Bake until lightly toasted, approximately 2½ minutes more. Let cool completely before crushing coconut with hands, the back of a spoon, or a mortar and pestle.
• In a medium bowl, whisk together flour, sugar, lemon zest, baking powder, salt, and cooled coconut. Using a pastry blender or 2 forks, cut butter into flour mixture until it resembles coarse crumbs.
• In a small bowl, stir together ¾ cup coconut milk and vanilla extract. Using a wooden spoon, stir coconut milk mixture into flour mixture until a soft dough forms.
• Turn out dough onto a lightly floured surface. Using a rolling pin, roll out dough to a 1-inch thickness. Using a 2-inch round cutter dipped in flour, cut 12 scones from dough without twisting cutter, rerolling scraps only once. Place scones 1 inch apart on prepared baking sheet.
• Brush tops of scones with remaining 2 tablespoons coconut milk.
• Bake until bottom edges of scones are light golden brown, 12 to 16 minutes. Let cool slightly. Serve warm.

RECOMMENDED CONDIMENTS:
Clotted cream | Strawberry preserves

Lemon-Walnut Scones

Makes 9

Fresh lemon zest and toasted walnuts form a delightful flavor duo in this enticing and toothsome bake, with the lemon notes reinforced by a little lemon extract.

2 cups all-purpose flour
¼ cup plus 1 teaspoon granulated sugar, divided
1 tablespoon fresh lemon zest
2 teaspoons baking powder
½ teaspoon fine sea salt
4 tablespoons cold unsalted butter, cubed
½ cup chopped toasted walnuts
¾ cup plus 1 tablespoon cold heavy whipping cream, divided
½ teaspoon lemon extract
¼ teaspoon vanilla extract

• Preheat oven to 350°. Line a rimmed baking sheet with parchment paper.
• In a large bowl, whisk together flour, ¼ cup sugar, lemon zest, baking powder, and salt. Using a pastry blender or 2 forks, cut butter into flour mixture until it resembles coarse crumbs. Stir in walnuts.
• In a liquid-measuring cup, stir together ¾ cup cream, lemon extract, and vanilla extract. Add to flour mixture, stirring until a shaggy dough begins to form. Working gently, bring mixture together in bowl with hands until a dough forms. (If dough won't come together, add more cream, 1 tablespoon at a time, until it does. Dough should be firm.)
• Turn out dough onto a lightly floured surface, and knead gently by patting dough and folding it in half 4 to 5 times. Using a rolling pin, roll out dough to a ¾-inch thickness. Using a 2¼-inch square cutter dipped in flour, cut 9 scones from dough without twisting cutter, rerolling scraps as necessary. Place scones 2 inches apart on prepared baking sheet.
• Brush tops of scones with remaining 1 tablespoon cream. Sprinkle tops of scones with remaining 1 tea-spoon sugar.
• Bake until edges of scones are golden brown, approxi-mately 20 minutes.

RECOMMENDED CONDIMENTS:
Clotted cream | Lemon curd

Zucchini-Walnut Scones
Makes 18

Two different kinds of flour, warming spices, fresh zucchini, toasted walnuts, and dried currants all meld together in this wholesome scone with nuances of salty and sweet.

2½ cups whole-wheat flour
1 cup all-purpose flour
⅓ cup firmly packed light brown sugar
1 tablespoon baking powder
½ teaspoon fine sea salt
½ teaspoon ground allspice
¼ teaspoon ground nutmeg
6 tablespoons cold unsalted butter, cubed
1 cup coarsely grated zucchini, squeezed dry
⅓ cup chopped toasted walnuts
⅓ cup dried currants
¾ cup cold heavy whipping cream
¼ cup whole milk
½ teaspoon vanilla extract

• Preheat oven to 350°. Line a rimmed baking sheet with parchment paper.
• In a large bowl, whisk together whole-wheat flour, all-purpose flour, brown sugar, baking powder, salt, allspice, and nutmeg. Using a pastry blender or 2 forks, cut butter into flour mixture until it resembles coarse crumbs. Stir in zucchini, walnuts, and currants.
• In a small bowl, stir together cream, milk, and vanilla extract. Add to flour mixture, stirring until a shaggy dough begins to form. Working gently, bring mixture together in bowl with hands until a dough forms. (If dough won't come together, add more cream, 1 table-spoon at a time, until it does. Dough should be firm.)
• Turn out dough onto a lightly floured surface, and knead gently until smooth by patting dough and folding it in half 4 to 5 times. Using a rolling pin, roll out dough to a ¾-inch thickness. Using a 2-inch fluted square cutter dipped in flour, cut 18 scones from dough without twisting cutter, rerolling scraps as necessary. Place scones 2 inches apart on prepared baking sheet.
• Bake until edges of scones are golden brown and a wooden pick inserted in the centers comes out clean, approximately 20 minutes. Serve warm or at room temperature.

RECOMMENDED CONDIMENT:
Creamy Brown Sugar Spread (recipe on page 125)

Fig & Walnut Scones

Makes 17

Dried figs and toasted walnuts add a terrific amount of sweetness and nuttiness to these harvest-inspired scones, while lemon zest and lemon extract provide unexpected, yet delicious, citrus notes.

2½ cups all-purpose flour
⅓ cup granulated sugar
1 tablespoon baking powder
1 tablespoon fresh lemon zest
½ teaspoon fine sea salt
6 tablespoons cold unsalted butter, cubed
½ cup chopped dried figs
⅓ cup chopped toasted walnuts
½ cup cold heavy whipping cream
½ teaspoon lemon extract
¼ teaspoon vanilla extract
2 large eggs, divided
1 tablespoon water

• Preheat oven to 375°. Line a rimmed baking sheet with parchment paper.
• In a large bowl, whisk together flour, sugar, baking powder, lemon zest, and salt. Using a pastry blender or 2 forks, cut butter into flour mixture until it resembles coarse crumbs. Stir in figs and walnuts.
• In a small bowl, whisk together cream, lemon extract, vanilla extract, and 1 egg. Add to flour mixture, stirring until a shaggy dough begins to form. Working gently, bring mixture together in bowl with hands until a dough forms. (If dough won't come together, add more cream, 1 tablespoon at a time, until it does. Dough should be firm.)
• Turn out dough onto a lightly floured surface, and knead gently until smooth by patting dough and folding it in half 4 to 5 times. Using a rolling pin, roll out dough to a ¾-inch thickness. Using a 2-inch round cutter dipped in flour, cut 17 scones from dough without twisting cutter, rerolling scraps as necessary. Place scones 2 inches apart on prepared baking sheet.
• In a small bowl, whisk together 1 tablespoon water and remaining 1 egg to make an egg wash. Brush tops of scones with egg wash.
• Bake until edges of scones are golden brown and a wooden pick inserted in the centers comes out clean, 18 to 20 minutes. Serve warm.

RECOMMENDED CONDIMENTS:
Clotted cream | Orange marmalade | Lemon curd

Hazelnut Scones
Makes 10

Delicately sweet and nutty, toasted hazelnuts impart rich taste to these plump scones that are best elevated by a healthy smothering of Faux Clotted Cream and a complementary hazelnut-chocolate spread of your choosing.

2 cups all-purpose flour
⅓ cup granulated sugar
2 teaspoons baking powder
½ teaspoon fine sea salt
4 tablespoons cold unsalted butter, cubed
⅓ cup chopped toasted hazelnuts
½ cup cold heavy whipping cream
¼ cup plus 3 tablespoons whole milk, divided
½ teaspoon vanilla extract
Garnish: blood orange slices

• Preheat oven to 350°. Line a rimmed baking sheet with parchment paper.
• In a large bowl, whisk together flour, sugar, baking powder, and salt. Using a pastry blender or 2 forks, cut butter into flour mixture until it resembles coarse crumbs. Stir in hazelnuts.
• In a small bowl, whisk together cream, ¼ cup plus 2 tablespoons milk, and vanilla extract. Add to flour mixture, stirring until a shaggy dough begins to form. Working gently, bring mixture together in bowl with hands until a dough forms. (If dough won't come together, add more cream, 1 tablespoon at a time, until it does. Dough should be firm.)
• Turn out dough onto a lightly floured surface, and knead gently until smooth by patting dough and folding it in half 4 to 5 times. Using a rolling pin, roll out dough to a 1-inch thickness. Using a 2-inch fluted square cutter dipped in flour, cut 10 scones from dough without twisting cutter, rerolling scraps as necessary. Place scones 2 inches apart on prepared baking sheet.
• Brush tops of scones with remaining 1 tablespoon milk.
• Bake until edges of scones are golden brown and a wooden pick inserted in the centers comes out clean, approximately 20 minutes.
• Garnish with blood orange slices, if desired.

RECOMMENDED CONDIMENTS:
Faux Clotted Cream (recipe on page 122) |
Hazelnut-chocolate spread

Apricot-Pistachio Scones
Makes 15

These toothsome scones perfectly combine sweet and salty with the addition of dried apricots and pistachios. Additionally, buttermilk gives the bakes nice flavor while also making them delightfully tender.

1¼ cups bread flour
1¼ cups cake flour
1 tablespoon granulated sugar
2 teaspoons baking powder
½ teaspoon fine sea salt
4 tablespoons plus 1 teaspoon cold unsalted butter, cubed
⅔ cup dried apricots, diced
⅓ cup toasted pistachios, finely chopped
½ cup plus 1 tablespoon whole buttermilk
2 large eggs, divided
1 teaspoon water

• Preheat oven to 375°. Line 2 rimmed baking sheets with parchment paper.
• In a large bowl, whisk together bread flour, cake flour, sugar, baking powder, and salt. Using a pastry blender or 2 forks, cut butter into flour mixture until it resembles coarse crumbs. Stir in apricots and pistachios.
• In a small bowl, whisk together buttermilk and 1 egg. Add to flour mixture, stirring until a shaggy dough begins to form. Working gently, bring mixture together in bowl with hands until a dough forms. (If dough won't come together, add more buttermilk, 1 tablespoon at a time, until it does. Dough should be firm.)
• Turn out dough onto a lightly floured surface, and knead gently until smooth by patting dough and folding it in half 5 to 7 times. Using a rolling pin, roll out dough to a ¾-inch thickness. Using a 2¼-inch round cutter dipped in flour, cut 15 scones from dough without twisting cutter, rerolling scraps as necessary.
• In a small bowl, whisk together 1 teaspoon water and remaining 1 egg to make an egg wash. Brush tops of scones with egg wash.
• Bake until edges of scones are golden brown and a wooden pick inserted in the centers comes out clean, 15 to 20 minutes. Serve warm.

RECOMMENDED CONDIMENTS:
Clotted cream | Orange marmalade

Orange-Pecan Scones
Makes approximately 9

Fantastically fluted round scones imparted with fresh orange zest, ground cardamom, and toasted pecans provide a heavenly first (or second) course for afternoon tea.

2 cups all-purpose flour
¼ cup plus 1 teaspoon granulated sugar, divided
2 teaspoons baking powder
2 teaspoons fresh orange zest
¾ teaspoon fine sea salt
½ teaspoon ground cardamom
6 tablespoons cold unsalted butter, cubed
½ cup finely chopped toasted pecans
⅔ cup plus 1 tablespoon cold heavy whipping cream, divided

• Preheat oven to 400°. Line a rimmed baking sheet with parchment paper.
• In a large bowl, whisk together flour, ¼ cup sugar, baking powder, orange zest, salt, and cardamom. Using a pastry blender or 2 forks, cut butter into flour mixture until it resembles coarse crumbs. Stir in pecans.
• Gradually add ⅔ cup cream to flour mixture, stirring just until a shaggy dough begins to form. Working gently, bring mixture together in bowl with hands until a dough forms. (If dough won't come together, add more cream, 1 tablespoon at a time, until it does. Dough should be somewhat firm.)
• Turn out dough onto a lightly floured surface, and knead gently until smooth by patting dough and folding it in half 4 to 5 times. Using a rolling pin, roll out dough to a 1-inch thickness. Using a 2¼-inch fluted round cutter dipped in flour, cut as many scones as possible from dough without twisting cutter, rerolling scraps once. Place scones 2 inches apart on prepared baking sheet.
• Brush tops of scones with remaining 1 tablespoon cream, and sprinkle tops of scones with remaining 1 teaspoon sugar.
• Bake until bottoms of scones are a deep golden brown, approximately 20 minutes. Serve warm.

RECOMMENDED CONDIMENTS:
Clotted cream | Orange marmalade

Raspberry-Orange Scones

Makes approximately 10

This recipe eliminates all doubt that fresh raspberries can be successfully incorporated into scones. The secret is to use firm raspberries, as they will not discolor the dough like soft ones will.

2¾ cup all-purpose flour
⅓ cup granulated sugar
1 tablespoon baking powder
1 teaspoon fine sea salt
8 tablespoons cold unsalted butter, cubed
1 cup whole milk
1 tablespoon fresh orange zest
½ teaspoon vanilla extract
⅓ cup fresh firm raspberries, gently broken into
   large pieces

• Preheat oven to 375°. Line a rimmed baking sheet with parchment paper.
• In a large bowl, whisk together flour, sugar, baking powder, and salt. Using a pastry blender or 2 forks, cut butter into flour mixture until it resembles coarse crumbs.
• In a medium bowl, whisk together milk, orange zest, and vanilla extract. Add to flour mixture, stirring gently until incorporated. Add raspberries, stirring very gently until incorporated. Working very gently, bring mixture together in bowl with hands until a dough forms.
• Turn out dough onto a lightly floured surface, and knead gently until smooth by patting dough and folding it in half 6 to 7 times. Using a rolling pin, roll out dough to a 1-inch thickness. Using a 2¼-inch round cutter dipped in flour, cut 10 scones from dough without twisting cutter, rerolling scraps no more than once. Place scones 2 inches apart on prepared baking sheet.
• Bake until edges of scones are lightly golden, 16 to 18 minutes. Let cool on baking sheet for 5 minutes.

RECOMMENDED CONDIMENTS:

Clotted cream | Orange marmalade

Raspberry–Poppy Seed Scones
Makes 16

Brimming with freeze-dried raspberries and poppy seeds, these sweet scones are lovely for a spring or summer teatime.

2¼ cups all-purpose flour
¼ cup granulated sugar
1 tablespoon baking powder
½ teaspoon poppy seeds
½ teaspoon fine sea salt
4 tablespoons cold unsalted butter, cubed
4 tablespoons cold cream cheese, cubed
1 cup plus 1 tablespoon freeze-dried raspberries, crushed
¾ cup plus 1 tablespoon cold heavy whipping cream, divided
1 large egg

• Preheat oven to 400°. Line a rimmed baking sheet with parchment paper.
• In a large bowl, whisk together flour, sugar, baking powder, poppy seeds, and salt. Using a pastry blender or 2 forks, cut butter and cream cheese into flour mixture until they resemble coarse crumbs. Stir in freeze-dried raspberries.
• Add ¾ cup cream to flour mixture, stirring until a shaggy dough begins to form. Working gently, bring mixture together in bowl with hands until a dough forms. (If dough won't come together, add more cream, 1 tablespoon at a time, until it does. Dough should be firm.)
• Turn out dough onto a lightly floured surface, and knead gently until smooth by patting dough and folding it in half 4 to 5 times. Using a rolling pin, roll out dough to a ½-inch thickness. Using a 2-inch fluted round cutter dipped in flour, cut 16 scones from dough without twisting cutter, rerolling scraps as necessary. Place scones, evenly spaced, on prepared baking sheet.
• In a small bowl, whisk together egg and remaining 1 tablespoon cream to make an egg wash. Brush tops of scones with egg wash.
• Bake until scones are lightly golden brown and a wooden pick inserted in the centers comes out clean, approximately 15 minutes. Serve warm.

RECOMMENDED CONDIMENTS:
Clotted cream | Lemon curd

Strawberry & Rose Water Scones
Makes 9

These pretty pink scones, with freeze-dried strawberries and a hint of rose water and vanilla extract, are delicious and fragrant.

2 cups all-purpose flour
⅓ cup granulated sugar
1 tablespoon baking powder
½ teaspoon fine sea salt
4 tablespoons cold unsalted butter, cubed
1 cup coarsely chopped freeze-dried strawberries
¾ cup plus 1 tablespoon cold heavy whipping cream, divided
2 teaspoons culinary rose water*
¼ teaspoon vanilla extract

• Preheat oven to 375°. Line a rimmed baking sheet with parchment paper.
• In a large bowl, whisk together flour, sugar, baking powder, and salt. Using a pastry blender or 2 forks, cut butter into flour mixture until it resembles coarse crumbs. Stir in strawberries.
• In a small bowl, stir together ¾ cup cream, rose water, and vanilla extract. Add to flour mixture, stirring until a shaggy dough begins to form. Working gently, bring mixture together in bowl with hands until a dough forms. (If dough won't come together, add more cream, 1 tablespoon at a time, until it does. Dough should be firm.)
• Turn out dough onto a lightly floured surface, and knead gently until smooth by patting dough and folding it in half 4 to 5 times. Using a rolling pin, roll out dough to a 1-inch thickness. Using a 2-inch round cutter dipped in flour, cut 9 scones from dough without twisting cutter, rerolling scraps as necessary. Place scones 2 inches apart on prepared baking sheet.
• Brush tops of scones with remaining 1 tablespoon cream.
• Bake until edges of scones are golden brown and a wooden pick inserted in the centers comes out clean, 17 to 20 minutes. Serve warm or at room temperature.

*We used Al Wadi Rose Water.

RECOMMENDED CONDIMENTS:
Clotted cream | Lemon curd

Rose Cream Scones
Makes 15

Heavy whipping cream gives these scones a lovely richness, and equal parts cake flour and all-purpose flour provide the tender crumb. High-quality rose water imparts light floral essence without being too perfumy.

1 cup all-purpose flour
1 cup cake flour
½ cup granulated sugar
2 teaspoons baking powder
½ teaspoon fine sea salt
¼ teaspoon cream of tartar
4 tablespoons cold salted butter, cubed
¾ cup plus 1 tablespoon cold heavy whipping cream
¼ teaspoon rose water*

• Preheat oven to 350°. Line a rimmed baking sheet with parchment paper.
• In a large bowl, whisk together all-purpose flour, cake flour, sugar, baking powder, salt, and cream of tartar. Using a pastry blender or 2 forks, cut butter into flour mixture until it resembles coarse crumbs.

• In a small bowl, stir together cream and rose water. Add to flour mixture, stirring until a shaggy dough begins to form. Working gently, bring mixture together in bowl with hands until a dough forms. (If dough won't come together, add more cream, 1 tablespoon at a time, until it does. Dough should be somewhat firm.)
• Turn out dough onto a lightly floured surface, and knead gently until smooth by patting dough and folding it in half 3 to 4 times. Using a rolling pin, roll out dough to a ½-inch thickness. Using a 2-inch fluted round cutter dipped in flour, cut 15 scones from dough without twisting cutter, rerolling scraps as necessary. Place scones 2 inches apart on prepared baking sheet.
• Bake until edges of scones are golden brown and a wooden pick inserted in the centers comes out clean, approximately 15 minutes.

We used Nielsen-Massey Rose Water.

RECOMMENDED CONDIMENT
Strawberry-Raspberry Quick Jam (page 128)

Jasmine Green Tea Scones

Makes 12

Laced with the sweet and floral fragrance of jasmine green tea leaves, these scones are light and bright morsels perfectly suited for any tea lover.

1 cup heavy whipping cream
4 tablespoons jasmine green tea leaves, divided
2 cups all-purpose flour
⅓ cup granulated sugar
2 teaspoons baking powder
½ teaspoon fine sea salt
4 tablespoons cold unsalted butter, cubed
½ teaspoon vanilla extract

• In a small saucepan, heat cream over medium-high heat until very hot, but not boiling. Remove from heat; add 2 tablespoons tea leaves. Cover, and let steep for 15 minutes. Strain cream though a fine-mesh sieve, and discard solids. Cover cream, and refrigerate until cold, 6 to 8 hours.
• Preheat oven to 350°. Line a rimmed baking sheet with parchment paper.
• Using a mortar and pestle or an electric spice grinder, grind remaining 2 tablespoons tea leaves.

• In a large bowl, whisk together ground tea leaves, flour, sugar, baking powder, and salt. Using a pastry blender or 2 forks, cut butter into flour mixture until it resembles coarse crumbs.
• Add vanilla extract to cold steeped cream, stirring well. Add to flour mixture, stirring until a shaggy dough begins to form. Working gently, bring mixture together in bowl with hands until a dough forms. (If dough won't come together, add more cream, 1 tablespoon at a time, until it does. Dough should be firm.)
• Turn out dough onto a lightly floured surface, and knead gently until smooth by patting dough and folding it in half 4 to 5 times. Using a rolling pin, roll out dough to a ¾-inch thickness. Using a 2-inch fluted round cutter dipped in flour, cut 12 scones from dough without twisting cutter, rerolling scraps as necessary. Place scones 2 inches apart on prepared baking sheet.
• Bake until edges of scones are golden brown and a wooden pick inserted in the centers comes out clean, approximately 20 minutes. Serve warm.

RECOMMENDED CONDIMENTS:

Clotted cream | Lemon curd

Strawberry, Lavender & White Chocolate Scones

Makes 12

Floral notes from dried lavender are perfectly balanced by the sweetness of white chocolate and strawberries in this tasty, heart-shaped scone. Using freeze-dried strawberries helps ensure that the dough does not have too much moisture, while still adding a refreshing berry flavor.

2 cups all-purpose flour
⅓ cup plus 1 tablespoon granulated sugar, divided
2 teaspoons baking powder
½ teaspoon dried culinary lavender
½ teaspoon fine sea salt
4 tablespoons cold salted butter, cubed
1 cup chopped freeze-dried strawberries
1 (4-ounce) bar white baking chocolate, chopped
1 cup cold heavy whipping cream
½ teaspoon vanilla extract

• Preheat oven to 350°. Line a rimmed baking sheet with parchment paper.
• In a large bowl, whisk together flour, ⅓ cup sugar, baking powder, lavender, and salt. Using a pastry blender or 2 forks, cut butter into flour mixture until it resembles coarse crumbs. Stir in strawberries and chocolate.
• In a liquid-measuring cup, stir together cream and vanilla extract. Add to flour mixture, stirring until a shaggy dough begins to form. Working gently, bring mixture together in bowl with hands until a dough forms. (If dough won't come together, add more cream, 1 tablespoon at a time, until it does. Dough should be firm.)
• Turn out dough onto a lightly floured surface, and knead gently by patting dough and folding it in half 4 to 5 times. Using a rolling pin, roll out dough to a ¾-inch thickness. Using a 3-inch heart-shaped cutter dipped in flour, cut 12 scones from dough without twisting cutter, rerolling scraps as necessary. Place scones 2 inches apart on prepared baking sheet.
• Sprinkle tops of scones with remaining 1 tablespoon sugar.
• Bake scones until edges are golden brown and a wooden pick inserted in the centers comes out clean, 18 to 20 minutes. Serve warm or at room temperature.

RECOMMENDED CONDIMENTS:
Clotted cream | Strawberry jam

Lemony White Chocolate Scones
Makes 15

The creamy yet gentle sweetness of white chocolate combines with bright lemon zest and lemon extract for a refreshing treat that is both sweet and tart.

2½ cups all-purpose flour
¼ cup granulated sugar
1 tablespoon baking powder
1 tablespoon fresh lemon zest
½ teaspoon fine sea salt
4 tablespoons cold salted butter, cubed
3 ounces white chocolate, finely chopped
1 cup plus 1 tablespoon cold heavy whipping cream,
    divided
½ teaspoon vanilla extract
⅛ teaspoon lemon extract
1 tablespoon sanding sugar

• Preheat oven to 375°. Line a rimmed baking sheet with parchment paper.
• In a large bowl, whisk together flour, sugar, baking powder, lemon zest, and salt. Using a pastry blender or 2 forks, cut butter into flour mixture until mixture resembles coarse crumbs. Stir in white chocolate.
• In a small bowl, whisk together 1 cup cream, vanilla extract, and lemon extract. Add to flour mixture, stirring until a shaggy dough begins to form. Working gently, bring mixture together in bowl with hands until a dough forms. (If dough won't come together, add more cream, 1 tablespoon at a time, until it does. Dough should be firm.)
• Turn out dough onto a lightly floured surface, and knead gently until smooth by patting dough and folding it in half 4 to 5 times. Using a rolling pin, roll out dough to a ¾-inch thickness. Using a 2-inch fluted round cutter dipped in flour, cut 15 scones from dough without twisting cutter, rerolling scraps as necessary. Place scones, evenly spaced, on prepared baking sheet.
• Brush tops of scones with remaining 1 tablespoon cream and sprinkle with sanding sugar.
• Bake until edges of scones are golden brown and a wooden pick inserted in the centers comes out clean, 16 to 18 minutes. Serve warm.

RECOMMENDED CONDIMENTS:
Strawberry preserves | Sweetened Whipped Cream (page 122)

Very Chocolaty Scones
Makes 12

These decadent scones, filled with three types of chocolate, are special treats for when you are craving something especially sweet.

2½ cups all-purpose flour
¼ cup granulated sugar
2 tablespoons firmly packed light brown sugar
1 tablespoon baking powder
½ teaspoon fine sea salt
4 tablespoons cold unsalted butter, cubed
⅓ cup semisweet chocolate morsels
¼ cup milk chocolate morsels
¼ cup chopped bittersweet chocolate baking bar
1¼ cups plus 1 tablespoon cold heavy whipping cream, divided
½ teaspoon vanilla extract

• Preheat oven to 375°. Line a rimmed baking sheet with parchment paper.
• In a large bowl, whisk together flour, both sugars, baking powder, and salt. Using a pastry blender or 2 forks, cut butter into flour mixture until it resembles coarse crumbs. Stir in chocolates.
• In a small bowl, stir together 1¼ cups cream and vanilla extract. Add to flour mixture, stirring until a shaggy dough begins to form. Working gently, bring mixture together in bowl with hands until a dough forms. (If dough won't come together, add more cream, 1 tablespoon at a time, until it does. Dough should be somewhat firm.)
• Turn out dough onto a lightly floured surface, and knead gently until smooth by patting dough and folding it in half 4 to 5 times. Using a rolling pin, roll out dough to a 1-inch thickness. Using a 2-inch round cutter dipped in flour, cut 12 scones from dough without twisting cutter, rerolling scraps as necessary. Place scones 2 inches apart on prepared baking sheet.
• Brush tops of scones with remaining 1 tablespoon cream.
• Bake until edges of scones are golden brown, 18 to 20 minutes. Serve warm.

RECOMMENDED CONDIMENTS:
Clotted cream | Strawberry preserves

Red Velvet Scones

Makes 12

These rich, scarlet-colored scones are a beautifully festive treat to serve for Valentine's Day or a bridal shower, and a dollop of Mascarpone Cream on top makes them especially decadent.

2 cups all-purpose flour
⅓ cup plus 2 tablespoons granulated sugar
¼ cup natural unsweetened cocoa powder
2 teaspoons baking powder
½ teaspoon fine sea salt
6 tablespoons cold salted butter, cubed
¾ cup cold heavy whipping cream
1 tablespoon red liquid food coloring
½ teaspoon vanilla extract
1 tablespoon white sparkling sugar

• Preheat oven to 350°. Spray the wells of 2 (6-well) heart-shaped baking pans* with nonstick cooking spray.
• In a large bowl, whisk together flour, sugar, cocoa powder, baking powder, and salt. Using a pastry blender or 2 forks, cut butter into flour mixture until it resembles coarse crumbs.
• In a liquid-measuring cup, whisk together cream, food coloring, and vanilla extract. Add to flour mixture, stirring to combine. Working gently, bring mixture together in bowl with hands until a dough forms and is evenly red.
• Using a levered 3-tablespoon scoop, divide dough evenly among wells of prepared pans. Pat dough into wells to create a level surface. Sprinkle scones with sparkling sugar.
• Bake until a wooden pick inserted in the centers comes out clean, approximately 15 minutes. Let cool in pans for 5 minutes. Remove scones from pan. Serve warm.

*We used Nordic Ware Platinum Mini Heart Baking Pans with 6 (½-cup) heart-shaped wells.

RECOMMENDED CONDIMENT:
Mascarpone Cream (recipe on page 124)

KITCHEN TIP: To prevent food coloring from staining hands, wear latex gloves when mixing dough.

2½ cups all-purpose flour
¼ cup granulated sugar
2½ teaspoons baking powder
½ teaspoon fine sea salt
8 tablespoons cold unsalted butter, cubed
¾ cup finely chopped dried apricots
⅓ cup finely chopped walnuts, toasted and cooled
⅓ cup miniature semisweet chocolate chips
1 cup plus 1 tablespoon cold heavy whipping cream,
   divided
1 large egg
½ teaspoon vanilla extract

• Preheat oven to 350°. Line a rimmed baking sheet
with parchment paper.
• In a large bowl, whisk together flour, sugar, baking
powder, and salt. Using a pastry blender or 2 forks,
cut butter into flour mixture until it resembles coarse
crumbs. Stir in apricots until coated with flour. Stir in
walnuts and chocolate chips.
• In a small bowl, whisk together 1 cup cream, egg,
and vanilla extract. Add to flour mixture, stirring until
a shaggy dough begins to form. Working gently, bring
mixture together in bowl with hands until a dough
forms. (If dough won't come together, add more cream,
1 tablespoon at a time, until it does. Dough should be firm.)
• Turn dough out onto a lightly floured surface, and
knead gently until smooth by patting dough and folding
it in half 4 to 5 times. Using a rolling pin, roll out dough
to a ¾-inch thickness. Using a 3¼-inch Star of David–
shaped cutter dipped in flour, cut as many scones as
possible from dough without twisting cutter, rerolling
scraps as necessary. Place scones 1 inch apart on prepared baking sheet. Place baking sheet with scones in
freezer for 15 minutes*.
• Brush tops of scones with remaining 1 tablespoon cream.
• Bake until edges of scones are golden brown, 20 to 25
minutes. Serve warm.

*At this point, scones can be frozen completely and then transferred to
an airtight freezer bag. Bake frozen scones without thawing, according
to recipe directions, within 3 months.

RECOMMENDED CONDIMENTS:
Sweetened Whipped Cream (recipe on page 122) | Apricot jam

Apricot, Chocolate & Walnut Scones
Makes 9 to 11

*The candied flavors of dried apricot and semisweet chocolate
pair wonderfully with bits of toasted walnut that are
incorporated into the dough of these scones. For a festive
look, be sure to use a Star of David–shaped cutter or one to
commemorate your holiday of choice.*

Chocolate-Hazelnut Scones

Makes 13

Bittersweet chocolate and toasted hazelnuts are the ideal sweet and savory combination for a scrumptious scone, especially when served with a dollop of Sweetened Whipped Cream.

2½ cups all-purpose flour
⅓ cup granulated sugar
1 tablespoon baking powder
½ teaspoon fine sea salt
4 tablespoons cold unsalted butter, cubed
1 (4-ounce) bar bittersweet chocolate, coarsely
    chopped
⅓ cup chopped toasted hazelnuts
½ cup plus 1 tablespoon cold heavy whipping cream,
    divided
½ cup whole milk
½ teaspoon vanilla extract

• Preheat oven to 350°. Line a rimmed baking sheet with parchment paper.
• In a large bowl, whisk together flour, sugar, baking powder, and salt. Using a pastry blender or 2 forks, cut in butter until it resembles coarse crumbs. Stir in chocolate and hazelnuts.
• In a small bowl, stir together ½ cup cream, milk, and vanilla extract. Add to flour mixture, stirring until a shaggy dough begins to form. Working gently, bring mixture together in bowl with hands until a dough forms. (If dough won't come together, add more cream, 1 tablespoon at a time, until it does. Dough should be firm.)
• Turn out dough onto a lightly floured surface, and knead gently by patting dough and folding it in half 4 to 5 times. Using a rolling pin, roll out dough to a 1-inch thickness. Using a 2½-inch round cutter dipped in flour, cut 13 scones from dough without twisting cutter, rerolling scraps as necessary. Place scones 2 inches apart on prepared baking sheet.
• Brush tops of scones with remaining 1 tablespoon cream.
• Bake until edges of scones are golden brown and a wooden pick inserted in the centers comes out clean, approximately 20 minutes. Serve warm.

RECOMMENDED CONDIMENT:
Sweetened Whipped Cream (recipe on page 122)

Dark Chocolate & Toasted Pecan Scones
Makes approximately 18

Bitter, yet incredibly tasty, dark chocolate chips bring out the nuttiness of chopped pecans in this decadent bake that positions the ingredients for scone perfection.

2 cups all-purpose flour
⅓ cup granulated sugar
2 teaspoons baking powder
½ teaspoon fine sea salt
8 tablespoons cold unsalted butter, cubed
½ cup dark chocolate chips
½ cup chopped toasted pecans
¾ cup cold heavy whipping cream
1 teaspoon vanilla extract

• Preheat oven to 400°. Line a a rimmed baking sheet with parchment paper.
• In large bowl, whisk together flour, sugar, baking powder, and salt. Using a pastry blender or 2 forks, cut butter into flour mixture until it resembles coarse crumbs. Stir in chocolate chips and pecans.
• In a liquid-measuring cup, stir together cream and vanilla extract. Add to flour mixture, stirring until a shaggy dough begins to form. Working gently, bring mixture together in bowl with hands until a dough forms. (If dough won't come together, add more cream, 1 tablespoon at a time, until it does. Dough should be firm.)
• Turn dough out onto a lightly floured surface, and knead gently until smooth by patting dough and folding it in half 3 to 4 times. Using a rolling pin, roll out dough to a 1-inch thickness. Using a 1¾-inch round cutter dipped in flour, cut as many scones as possible from dough without twisting cutter, rerolling scraps as necessary. Place scones 2 inches apart on prepared baking sheet. Refrigerate until chilled, approximately 10 minutes.
• Bake until scones are lightly browned, approximately 17 minutes. Serve warm.

RECOMMENDED CONDIMENTS:
Clotted cream | Strawberry-champagne jam

Pear, Pancetta & Pecan Scones
Makes 12

Ripe pear, savory pancetta, and nutty pecans, plus the spicy notes of mace and black pepper, give this sweet scone contrasting flavors that work so well together. Offer guests a complementary honey-sweetened homemade mascarpone cheese spread.

2½ cups all-purpose flour
¼ cup granulated sugar
1 tablespoon baking powder
½ teaspoon fine sea salt
¼ teaspoon ground mace
⅛ teaspoon ground black pepper
4 tablespoons cold unsalted butter, cubed
½ cup diced peeled firm ripe pear
⅓ cup chopped toasted pecans
⅓ cup coarsely chopped cooked pancetta
½ cup plus 1 tablespoon cold heavy whipping cream, divided
2 large eggs, divided
½ teaspoon vanilla extract

• Preheat oven to 375°. Line a rimmed baking sheet with parchment paper.
• In a large bowl, whisk together flour, sugar, baking powder, salt, mace, and pepper. Using a pastry blender or 2 forks, cut butter into flour mixture until it resembles coarse crumbs. Stir in pear, pecans, and pancetta.
• In a small bowl, whisk together ½ cup cream, 1 egg, and vanilla extract. Add to flour mixture, stirring until a shaggy dough begins to form. Working gently, bring mixture together in bowl with hands until a dough forms. (If dough won't come together, add more cream, 1 tablespoon at a time, until it does. Dough should be firm.)
• Turn out dough onto a lightly floured surface, and knead gently until smooth by patting dough and folding it in half 3 to 4 times. Using a rolling pin, roll out dough to a ¾-inch thickness. Using a 2-inch fluted round cutter dipped in flour, cut 12 scones from dough without twisting cutter, rerolling scraps as necessary. Place scones 2 inches apart on prepared baking sheet.
• In a small bowl, whisk together remaining 1 tablespoon cream and remaining 1 egg to make an egg wash. Brush tops of scones with egg wash.

• Bake until edges of scones are golden brown and a wooden pick inserted in the centers comes out clean, 18 to 20 minutes. Serve warm.

RECOMMENDED CONDIMENT:
Honey-Mascarpone Cream (recipe on page 124)

Black Walnut–Butterscotch Scones
Makes 11

Toasted black walnuts give these scones added crunch and a delightful earthy flavor that pairs wonderfully with sweeter ingredients like butterscotch chips.

2½ cups all-purpose flour
¼ cup granulated sugar
1 tablespoon baking powder
½ teaspoon fine sea salt
4 tablespoons cold unsalted butter, cubed
½ cup butterscotch chips
½ cup chopped black walnuts, toasted
1 cup plus 1 tablespoon cold heavy whipping cream, divided
½ teaspoon vanilla extract
Garnish: turbinado sugar

• Preheat oven to 375°. Line a rimmed baking sheet with parchment paper.
• In a large bowl, whisk together flour, sugar, baking powder, and salt. Using a pastry blender or 2 forks, cut butter into flour mixture until it resembles coarse crumbs. Stir in butterscotch chips and walnuts.
• In a small bowl, stir together 1 cup cream and vanilla extract. Add cream mixture to flour mixture, stirring until a shaggy dough begins to form. Working gently, bring mixture together in bowl with hands until a dough forms. (If dough won't come together, add more cream, 1 tablespoon at a time, until it does. Dough should be firm.)
• Turn out dough onto a lightly floured surface, and knead gently until smooth by patting dough and folding it in half 4 to 5 times. Using a rolling pin, roll out dough to a ¾-inch thickness. Using a 2½-inch round cutter dipped in flour, cut 11 scones from dough without twisting cutter, rerolling scraps as necessary. Place scones 2 inches apart on prepared baking sheet.
• Brush tops of scones with remaining 1 tablespoon cream. Garnish tops of scones with a sprinkle of turbinado sugar, if desired.
• Bake until edges of scones are golden brown and a wooden pick inserted in the centers comes out clean, 20 to 23 minutes. Serve warm.

RECOMMENDED CONDIMENTS:
Clotted cream | Pumpkin butter

Peanut Butter Scones
Makes 19

Paired with strawberry jam, these scrumptious scones, which get their peanut butter taste from morsels, might very well remind you of your childhood.

2 cups all-purpose flour
⅓ cup granulated sugar
2 teaspoons baking powder
½ teaspoon fine sea salt
4 tablespoons cold salted butter, cubed
½ cup peanut butter morsels
1 cup plus 1 tablespoon cold heavy whipping cream, divided
½ teaspoon vanilla extract
Garnish: turbinado sugar

• Preheat oven to 350°. Line 2 rimmed baking sheets with parchment paper.
• In a large bowl, whisk together flour, sugar, baking powder, and salt. Using a pastry blender or 2 forks, cut butter into flour mixture until it resembles coarse crumbs. Stir in peanut butter morsels.
• In a small bowl, stir together 1 cup cream and vanilla extract. Add to flour mixture, stirring until a shaggy dough begins to form. Working gently, bring mixture together in bowl with hands until a dough forms. (If dough won't come together, add more cream, 1 tablespoon at a time, until it docs. Dough should be somewhat firm.)
• Turn out dough onto a lightly floured surface, and knead gently until smooth by patting dough and folding it in half 4 to 5 times. Using a rolling pin, roll out dough to a ½-inch thickness. Using a 2½-inch triangular cutter dipped in flour, cut 19 shapes from dough without twisting cutter, rerolling scraps as necessary. Place scones 2 inches apart on prepared baking sheets.
• Brush tops of scones with remaining 1 tablespoon cream. Garnish tops of scones with a sprinkle of turbinado sugar, if desired.
• Bake until edges of scones are golden brown and a wooden pick inserted in the centers comes out clean, approximately 20 minutes.

RECOMMENDED CONDIMENTS:
Clotted cream | Strawberry jam

Snickerdoodle Scones

Makes 14

Celebrate the cooler weather of autumn and winter with this scrumptious twist on a classic, spice-filled cookie.

2½ cups all-purpose flour
⅓ cup plus 2 tablespoons granulated sugar, divided
1 tablespoon baking powder
2 tablespoons plus 1 teaspoon ground cinnamon, divided
½ teaspoon fine sea salt
6 tablespoons cold unsalted butter, cubed
1 cup plus 2 tablespoons cold heavy whipping cream, divided
½ teaspoon vanilla extract

• Preheat oven to 350°. Line a rimmed baking sheet with parchment paper.
• In a large bowl, whisk together flour, ⅓ cup sugar, baking powder, 1 teaspoon cinnamon, and salt. Using a pastry blender or 2 forks, cut butter into flour mixture until it resembles coarse crumbs.

• In a small bowl, whisk together 1 cup cream and vanilla extract. Add to flour mixture, stirring until a shaggy dough begins to form. Working gently, bring mixture together in bowl with hands until a dough forms. (If dough won't come together, add more cream, 1 table-spoon at a time, until it does. Dough should be firm.)
• Turn out dough onto a lightly floured surface, and knead gently until smooth by patting dough and folding it in half 4 to 5 times. Using a rolling pin, roll out dough to a ¾-inch thickness. Using a 2½-inch fluted round cutter dipped in flour, cut 14 scones from dough without twisting cutter, rerolling scraps as necessary. Place scones 2 inches apart on prepared baking sheet.
• Brush tops of scones with remaining 2 tablespoons cream.
• In a small bowl, whisk together remaining 2 table-spoons sugar and remaining 2 tablespoons cinnamon. Sprinkle cinnamon sugar over tops of scones.
• Bake until edges of scones are golden brown and a wooden pick inserted in the centers comes out clean, approximately 20 minutes. Serve warm.

RECOMMENDED CONDIMENTS:
Clotted cream | Apple jelly | Strawberry preserves

Spiced Cream Cheese Scones
Makes 18

This intriguing bake, filled with an array of seasonings—from cinnamon and cloves to nutmeg and ginger—is delightfully nuanced. The dough is made with bread flour and balanced with a little cake flour for best texture, with cream cheese adding marvelous richness.

2 cups bread flour
¼ cup cake flour
½ cup granulated sugar
2½ teaspoons baking powder
½ teaspoon fine sea salt
½ teaspoon ground cinnamon, divided
½ teaspoon ground cloves, divided
½ teaspoon ground allspice, divided
½ teaspoon ground nutmeg, divided
½ teaspoon ground ginger, divided
4 tablespoons cold unsalted butter, cubed
4 ounces cold cream cheese, cubed
1 cup plus 2 tablespoons cold heavy whipping cream, divided

• Preheat oven to 400°. Line 2 rimmed baking sheets with parchment paper.
• In a medium bowl, whisk together bread flour, cake flour, sugar, baking powder, salt, ¼ teaspoon cinnamon, ¼ teaspoon cloves, ¼ teaspoon allspice, ¼ teaspoon nutmeg, and ¼ teaspoon ginger. Using a pastry blender or 2 forks, cut in butter and cream cheese until they resemble coarse crumbs.
• Add 1 cup cream to flour mixture, stirring until a shaggy dough begins to form. Working gently, bring mixture together in bowl with hands until a dough forms. (If dough won't come together, add more cream, 1 table-spoon at a time, until it does. Dough should be firm.)
• Turn out dough onto a lightly floured surface, and knead gently until smooth by patting dough and folding it in half 5 to 7 times. Using a rolling pin, roll out dough to a ½-inch thickness. Using a 2-inch fluted round cut-ter dipped in flour, cut 18 scones from dough without twisting cutter, rerolling scraps as necessary. Place scones 2 inches apart on prepared baking sheets.
• In a small bowl, whisk together remaining 2 tablespoons cream, remaining ¼ teaspoon cinnamon, remaining ¼ teaspoon cloves, remaining ¼ teaspoon allspice, remaining ¼ teaspoon nutmeg, and remaining ¼ tea-spoon ginger. Brush tops of scones with cream mixture.

• Bake until edges of scones are golden brown and a wooden pick inserted in the centers comes out clean, 12 to 15 minutes. Serve warm.

RECOMMENDED CONDIMENTS:
Clotted cream | Orange-cranberry marmalade

Cinnamon-Currant Scones
Makes 12

Tiny, dried currants mingle with ground cinnamon to create a tremendous scone that is enjoyable to serve during the holiday season. If dried currants are not available, use an equal amount of chopped raisins instead.

3 cups all-purpose flour
⅓ cup granulated sugar
4 teaspoons baking powder
1½ teaspoons ground cinnamon
½ teaspoon fine sea salt
8 tablespoons cold unsalted butter, cubed
½ cup dried currants
1 cup plus 1 tablespoon cold heavy whipping cream, divided
1 large egg
Garnish: sparkling sugar

• Preheat oven to 400°. Line a rimmed baking sheet with parchment paper.
• In a large bowl, whisk together flour, granulated sugar, baking powder, cinnamon, and salt. Using a pastry blender or 2 forks, cut in butter until it resembles coarse crumbs. Stir in currants.
• Add 1 cup cream to flour mixture, stirring with a fork just until a shaggy dough begins to form. Working gently, bring mixture together in bowl with hands until a dough forms. (If dough won't come together, add more cream, 1 tablespoon at a time, until it does. Dough should be firm.)
• Turn out dough onto a lightly floured surface, and knead gently until smooth by patting dough and folding it in half 4 to 5 times. Cover and let rest at room temperature for 15 minutes. Using a rolling pin, roll out dough to a ¾-inch thickness. Using a 2¼-inch fluted round cutter dipped in flour, cut 12 scones from dough without twisting cutter, rerolling scraps as necessary. Place scones 2 inches apart on prepared baking sheet.
• In a small bowl, whisk together egg and remaining 1 tablespoon cream to make an egg wash. Brush tops of scones with egg wash. Garnish tops with a sprinkle of sparkling sugar, if desired.
• Bake until tops of scones are golden and a wooden pick inserted in the centers comes out clean, 12 to 15 minutes. Serve warm.

RECOMMENDED CONDIMENTS:
Clotted cream | Seedless blackberry jam

Cinnamon Scones

Makes 12

These tempting scones are studded with sweet cinnamon morsels for a delicious burst of spice in each bite.

2 cups all-purpose flour
1/3 cup granulated sugar
2 teaspoons baking powder
1/2 teaspoon fine sea salt
4 tablespoons cold salted butter, cubed
3/4 cup cinnamon morsels*
3/4 cup plus 2 tablespoons cold heavy whipping cream
1/2 teaspoon vanilla extract
Garnish: turbinado sugar

• Preheat oven to 350°. Line a rimmed baking sheet with parchment paper.
• In a large bowl, whisk together flour, granulated sugar, baking powder, and salt. Using a pastry blender or 2 forks, cut butter into flour mixture until it resembles coarse crumbs. Stir in cinnamon morsels.

• In a small bowl, stir together cream and vanilla extract. Add to flour mixture, stirring until a shaggy dough begins to form. Working gently, bring mixture together in bowl with hands until a dough forms. (If dough won't come together, add more cream, 1 tablespoon at a time, until it does. Dough should be firm.)
• Turn out dough onto a lightly floured surface, and knead gently by patting dough and folding it in half 4 to 5 times. Using a rolling pin, roll out dough to a 1/2-inch thickness. Using a 3 1/4-inch triangular-shaped cutter dipped in flour, cut 12 scones from dough without twisting cutter, rerolling scraps as necessary. Place scones 2 inches apart on prepared baking sheet.
• Garnish scones with a sprinkle of turbinado sugar, if desired.
• Bake until edges of scones are golden brown and a wooden pick inserted in the centers comes out clean, approximately 20 minutes. Serve warm.

We used Hershey's Cinnamon Baking Chips.

RECOMMENDED CONDIMENTS:
Clotted cream | Apple butter

Cinnamon Roll Scones
Makes 12

This twist on a beloved breakfast treat makes the perfect addition to a cozy teatime at any time of the day. And because it sports a tasty icing, no other condiments are necessary.

2 cups all-purpose flour
¼ cup granulated sugar
1 tablespoon baking powder
½ teaspoon baking soda
¼ teaspoon fine sea salt
8 tablespoons cold unsalted butter, cubed
½ cup cold whole buttermilk
2 tablespoons unsalted butter, melted and divided
¼ cup firmly packed light brown sugar
¼ cup chopped lightly toasted pecans
¼ cup raisins
1½ tablespoons ground cinnamon
Cinnamon Roll Icing (recipe follows)

• Preheat oven to 375°. Line a rimmed baking sheet with parchment paper.
• In a large bowl, whisk together flour, sugar, baking powder, baking soda, and salt. Using a pastry blender or 2 forks, cut butter into flour mixture until it resembles coarse crumbs.
• Add buttermilk to flour mixture, stirring until a shaggy dough begins to form. Working gently, bring mixture together in bowl with hands until a dough forms. (If dough won't come together, add more buttermilk, 1 tablespoon at a time, until it does. Dough should be somewhat firm.)
• Turn out dough onto a lightly floured surface, and knead gently until smooth by patting dough and folding it in half 5 to 7 times. Using a rolling pin, roll out dough to a 12x7-inch (½-inch-thick) rectangle.
• Brush dough with 1 tablespoon melted butter.
• In a medium bowl, stir together brown sugar, pecans, raisins, and cinnamon until combined. Sprinkle brown sugar mixture evenly over dough. Roll up dough lengthwise, keeping a tight spiral.
• Using a sharp knife, trim and discard ends of roll, creating a 12-inch log. Cut log into 12 slices (scones). Place scones ½ inch apart on prepared baking sheet. Freeze for 10 minutes.
• Brush scones with remaining 1 tablespoon melted butter.
• Bake until edges of scones are golden brown, 14 to 16 minutes.

• Drizzle scones with Cinnamon Roll Icing. Serve warm or at room temperature.

Cinnamon Roll Icing
Makes approximately ½ cup

This luscious icing can be drizzled on our Cinnamon Roll Scones for an eye-catching presentation or can be spread using a spatula for a thick and even coating.

1 cup confectioners' sugar
2 tablespoons half-and-half
1 tablespoon unsalted butter, softened
½ teaspoon vanilla extract

• In a medium bowl, whisk together confectioners' sugar, half-and-half, butter, and vanilla extract until smooth. (If necessary, add more half-and-half to achieve desired consistency.) Use immediately.

Carrot Cake Scones
Makes 16

This recipe reimagines a classic springtime dessert by combining the delicious flavors of carrots, golden raisins, pecans, and spices like cinnamon, ginger, and allspice. A dollop of Cream Cheese Spread, in lieu of clotted cream, is an ideal finishing touch.

3 cups all-purpose flour
½ cup granulated sugar
1 tablespoon baking powder
1 teaspoon ground cinnamon
¾ teaspoon fine sea salt
½ teaspoon ground ginger
¼ teaspoon ground allspice
8 tablespoons cold unsalted butter, cubed
1 cup finely grated carrot
⅓ cup golden raisins
⅓ cup chopped pecans
1 cup cold heavy whipping cream
1 large egg, lightly beaten

• Line a rimmed baking sheet with parchment paper.
• In a large bowl, whisk together flour, sugar, baking powder, cinnamon, salt, ginger, and allspice. Using a pastry blender or 2 forks, cut butter into flour mixture

until it resembles coarse crumbs. Cover and freeze for 15 minutes. Stir in carrot, raisins, and pecans.
• Add cream to flour mixture, stirring until a shaggy dough begins to form. Working gently, bring mixture together in bowl with hands until a dough forms. (If dough won't come together, add more cream, 1 tablespoon at a time, until it does.)
• Turn out dough onto a heavily floured surface. Using well-floured hands, knead gently until smooth by patting dough and folding it in half 10 to 15 times. Pat out dough to a ¾-inch thickness. Using 2-inch round cutter dipped in flour, cut 16 scones from dough without twisting cutter, rerolling scraps as necessary. Place scones approximately 1½ inches apart on prepared baking sheet. Freeze for 15 minutes.
• Meanwhile, preheat oven to 400°.
• Brush tops of cold scones with beaten egg.
• Bake until scones are golden brown, 16 to 19 minutes. Let cool slightly before serving.

RECOMMENDED CONDIMENT
Cream Cheese Spread (page 122)

Sweet Potato–Ginger Scones
Makes 20

If you are searching for the ultimate scone to serve at a fall fête or Thanksgiving celebration, look no further than these oh-so comforting morsels that get their piquant notes from fresh ginger and are only made better by a dollop of piped clotted cream.

2½ cups all-purpose flour
2 tablespoons granulated sugar
2 tablespoons firmly packed light brown sugar
1 tablespoon baking powder
1 teaspoon ground cinnamon
½ teaspoon grated fresh ginger
½ teaspoon fine sea salt
8 tablespoons cold unsalted butter, cubed
¾ cup cold mashed baked sweet potato
    (approximately 1 large sweet potato)
⅔ cup plus 1 tablespoon cold heavy whipping cream,
    divided
2 tablespoons ginger cane sugar

• Preheat oven to 400°. Line 2 rimmed baking sheets with parchment paper.
• In a large bowl, whisk together flour, granulated sugar, brown sugar, baking powder, cinnamon, ginger, and salt. Using a pastry blender or 2 forks, cut in butter until it resembles coarse crumbs.
• In a medium bowl, stir together mashed sweet potato and ⅔ cup cream. Add to flour mixture, stirring until a shaggy dough begins to form. Working gently, bring mixture together in bowl with hands until a dough forms. (If dough won't come together, add more cream, 1 tablespoon at a time, until it does. Dough should be somewhat firm.)
• Turn out dough onto a lightly floured surface, and knead gently until smooth by patting dough and folding it in half 4 to 5 times. Using a rolling pin, roll out dough to a ½-inch thickness. Using a 2¼-inch fluted round cutter dipped in flour, cut 20 scones from dough with-out twisting cutter, rerolling scraps as necessary. Place scones 1 inch apart on prepared baking sheets.
• Brush tops of scones with remaining 1 tablespoon cream, and sprinkle with ginger cane sugar.

- Bake until edges of scones are golden brown and a wooden pick inserted in the centers comes out clean, approximately 12 minutes. Serve warm.

RECOMMENDED CONDIMENTS:
Clotted cream | Orange marmalade

KITCHEN TIP: To make purchased clotted cream look especially pretty, let it come to room temperature, transfer it to a piping bag fitted with a rose tip (Ateco #125), and pipe it into a serving bowl. Cover gently with plastic wrap and refrigerate until needed.

Sweet Potato–Raisin Scones
Makes 12

Apple pie spice, red raisins, chopped hazelnuts, and grated sweet potato have these scones brimming with rich, autumnal flavor.

3 cups all-purpose flour
½ cup granulated sugar
1 tablespoon baking powder
1½ teaspoons apple pie spice
½ teaspoon fine sea salt
8 tablespoons cold unsalted butter, cubed
½ cup finely grated sweet potato
⅓ cup red raisins
⅓ cup chopped hazelnuts
1 cup heavy whipping cream
1 large egg, lightly beaten

- Line a rimmed baking sheet with parchment paper.
- In a large bowl, whisk together flour, sugar, baking powder, apple pie spice, and salt. Using a pastry blender or 2 forks, cut butter into flour mixture until it resembles coarse crumbs. Cover flour mixture and freeze for 15 minutes. Stir in sweet potato, raisins, and hazelnuts.
- Add cream to flour mixture, stirring until mixture is evenly moist.
- Turn out dough onto a heavily floured surface, and knead gently until smooth by patting dough and folding it in half 10 to 15 times. Using a rolling pin, roll out dough to a ¾-inch thickness. Using a 2-inch round cutter dipped in flour, cut 12 scones from dough without twisting cutter, rerolling scraps as necessary. Place scones 1½ inches apart on prepared baking sheet. Freeze for 15 minutes.
- Meanwhile, preheat oven to 400°.
- Brush tops of scones with beaten egg.
- Bake until edges of scones are golden brown and a wooden pick inserted in the centers comes out clean, 16 to 19 minutes. Serve warm.

RECOMMENDED CONDIMENTS:
Clotted cream | Orange marmalade

Butternut Squash Scones
Makes 16

Laden with roasted butternut squash and the perfect amount of fresh sage, these superbly golden scones evoke the beloved flavors and colors of the autumnal season.

1 small (approximately 1 pound) butternut squash
2 cups all-purpose flour
¼ cup plus 2 tablespoons granulated sugar
1 tablespoon baking powder
1 tablespoon chopped fresh sage
½ teaspoon fine sea salt
½ teaspoon ground cinnamon
8 tablespoons cold unsalted butter, cubed
¼ cup plus 1 tablespoon cold heavy whipping cream, divided
1 large egg
2 tablespoons cane sugar

• Preheat oven to 400°. Line a rimmed baking sheet with foil.
• Using a large sharp knife, cut squash in half lengthwise. Using a spoon, scoop out and discard seeds. Place squash halves, cut sides down, on prepared baking sheet. Pierce top side of squash several times with a fork.
• Bake until squash is tender, 35 to 40 minutes. Let cool for 10 minutes.
• Peel and discard skin from squash.

• In a large bowl, mash squash pulp with a fork until smooth. Cover and refrigerate until chilled, approximately 30 minutes.
• Line another rimmed baking sheet with parchment paper.
• In the work bowl of a food processor, pulse together flour, granulated sugar, baking powder, sage, salt, and cinnamon until combined. Add butter, pulsing until it resembles coarse crumbs. Transfer mixture to a large bowl.
• Add squash and ¼ cup cream to flour mixture, stirring until a dough forms.
• Turn out dough onto a lightly floured surface, and knead gently until smooth by patting dough and folding it in half 5 to 7 times. Using a rolling pin, roll out dough to a ¾-inch thickness. Using a 2-inch fluted round cutter dipped in flour, cut 16 scones from dough without twisting cutter, rerolling scraps as necessary. Place scones 2 inches apart on prepared baking sheet. Place baking sheet in freezer for 10 minutes.
• In a small bowl, whisk together egg and remaining 1 tablespoon cream to make an egg wash. Brush tops of scones with egg wash, and sprinkle with cane sugar.
• Bake until edges of scones are golden brown and a wooden pick inserted in the centers comes out clean, 15 to 18 minutes. Serve warm.

RECOMMENDED CONDIMENT:
Clotted cream

Caramel-Apple Scones
Makes 15

Tart Granny Smith apple, warming cinnamon, and a marvelous Caramel Glaze combine for a festive scone perfect for fall.

7 tablespoons cold unsalted butter, cubed, divided
1¼ cups peeled, cored, and diced Granny Smith apple
⅓ cup plus 1 tablespoon granulated sugar, divided
⅛ teaspoon ground cinnamon
3 cups all-purpose flour
1 tablespoon baking powder
¾ teaspoon fine sea salt
1 cup plus 2 tablespoons cold heavy whipping cream
½ teaspoon vanilla extract
Caramel Glaze (recipe follows)
Garnish: chopped toasted pecans and flaked salt

- In a medium nonstick sauté pan, melt 1 tablespoon butter over medium-high heat. Add apples, and sprinkle with 1 tablespoon sugar and cinnamon, stirring well. Cook until apples are just beginning to become tender, 1 to 2 minutes. Let cool completely. (It is important for apples to be completely cooled before using.)
- Preheat oven to 350°. Line a rimmed baking sheet with parchment paper.
- In a large bowl, whisk together flour, baking powder, salt, and remaining ⅓ cup sugar. Using a pastry blender or 2 forks, cut remaining 6 tablespoons butter into flour mixture until it resembles coarse crumbs. Stir in cooled apple mixture.
- In a small bowl, stir together cream and vanilla extract. Add to flour mixture, stirring until a shaggy dough begins to form. Working gently, bring mixture together in bowl with hands until a dough forms. (If dough won't come together, add more cream, 1 tablespoon at a time, until it does. Dough should be firm.)
- Turn out dough onto a lightly floured surface, and knead gently by patting dough and folding it in half 4 to 5 times. Using a rolling pin, roll out dough to a 1-inch thickness. Using a 2¼-inch round cutter dipped in flour, cut 15 scones from dough without twisting cutter, rerolling scraps as necessary. Place scones 2 inches apart on prepared baking sheet.
- Bake until edges of scones are golden brown and a wooden pick inserted in the centers comes out clean, approximately 20 minutes. Let cool, if desired.
- Top scones with Caramel Glaze. (Glaze can be applied when scones are warm or cool, but if scones are warm, glaze will run.)
- While glaze is warm, garnish scones with pecans and flaked salt, if desired.

Caramel Glaze
Makes 1 cup

This decadent glaze is the perfect way to add an extra bit of richness to your favorite scones. You can also adjust the consistency by adding more milk for a runnier glaze that is easy to drizzle over the top, or increasing the amount of confectioners' sugar for a thicker caramel coating.

½ cup unsalted butter
½ cup firmly packed light brown sugar
¼ cup whole milk
1 cup sifted confectioners' sugar
½ teaspoon vanilla extract

- In a small saucepan, melt butter over medium heat. Stir in brown sugar and milk. Bring to a boil over medium heat, stirring constantly. Cook for exactly 2 minutes. Remove from heat.
- Whisk in confectioners' sugar and vanilla extract until incorporated. (Adjust thickness of glaze by adding more confectioners' sugar or milk, a little at a time.) Use immediately.

and salt. Using a pastry blender or 2 forks, cut butter into flour mixture until it resembles coarse crumbs.
• In a small bowl, whisk together ½ cup plus 2 tablespoons cream and egg. Add to flour mixture, stirring until a shaggy dough begins to form. Working gently, bring mixture together in bowl with hands until a dough forms. (If dough won't come together, add more cream, 1 tablespoon at a time, until it does. Dough should be somewhat firm.)
• Turn out dough onto a lightly floured surface, and knead gently until smooth by patting dough and folding it in half 4 to 5 times. Using a rolling pin, roll out dough to a ¾-inch thickness. Using a 2-inch square cutter dipped in flour, cut 12 scones from dough without twisting cutter, rerolling scraps as necessary. Place scones 2 inches apart on prepared baking sheet.
• Brush tops of scones with remaining 1 tablespoon cream, and sprinkle with remaining 2 tablespoons oats.
• Bake until edges of scones are golden brown and a wooden pick inserted in the centers comes out clean, approximately 12 minutes. Serve warm.

RECOMMENDED CONDIMENTS:
Clotted cream | Red currant jam

Oat & Wheat Scones
Makes 12

The addition of whole-wheat flour and oats to the dough of these toothsome scones gives them a delightful crunch and lovely texture, while light brown sugar provides the desired sweetness.

1 cup whole-wheat flour
½ cup all-purpose flour
½ cup plus 2 tablespoons quick-cooking oats, divided
⅓ cup firmly packed light brown sugar
2 teaspoons baking powder
½ teaspoon fine sea salt
6 tablespoons cold salted butter, cubed
½ cup plus 3 tablespoons cold heavy whipping cream, divided
1 large egg

• Preheat oven to 400°. Line a rimmed baking sheet with parchment paper.
• In a large bowl, whisk together whole-wheat flour, all-purpose flour, ½ cup oats, brown sugar, baking powder,

Multiseed Scones
Makes 11

These golden-brown scones include a wonderful assortment of seeds—sesame, poppy, flax, and sunflower—in both the dough and the sprinkled topping. Spelt flour, in lieu of all-purpose flour, adds noticeable taste to enhance the overall flavor.

2½ cups spelt flour
¼ cup firmly packed light brown sugar
4 tablespoons chopped roasted salted sunflower seeds, divided
3 tablespoons flax seeds, divided
1 tablespoon toasted sesame seeds
1 tablespoon baking powder
½ teaspoon fine sea salt
6 tablespoons cold unsalted butter, cubed
1 cup cold heavy whipping cream
1 large egg white, lightly beaten
1 tablespoon sesame seeds
1 teaspoon poppy seeds

• Preheat oven to 375°. Line a rimmed baking sheet with parchment paper.

• In a large bowl, whisk together flour, brown sugar, 3 tablespoons sunflower seeds, 2 tablespoons flax seeds, toasted sesame seeds, baking powder, and salt. Using a pastry blender or 2 forks, cut in butter until it resembles coarse crumbs.

• Add cream to flour mixture, stirring until a shaggy dough begins to form. Working gently, bring mixture together in bowl with hands until a dough forms. (If dough won't come together, add more cream, 1 table-spoon at a time, until it does. Dough should be firm.)

• Turn out dough onto a lightly floured surface (spelt flour), and knead gently until smooth by patting dough and folding it in half 4 to 5 times. Using a rolling pin, roll out dough to a 1-inch thickness. Using a 2¼-inch round cutter dipped in flour, cut 11 scones from dough without twisting cutter, rerolling scraps as necessary. Place scones 2 inches apart on prepared baking sheet.

• Brush tops of scones with egg white.

• In a small bowl, stir together sesame seeds, poppy seeds, remaining 1 tablespoon flax seeds, and remain-ing 1 tablespoon sunflower seeds. Sprinkle mixture onto tops of scones.

• Bake until edges of scones are golden brown and a wooden pick inserted in the centers comes out clean, approximately 21 minutes. Serve warm.

RECOMMENDED CONDIMENTS:
Clotted cream | Mixed-berry preserves

DATE, CHIVE &
PARMESAN SCONES,
page 90

SAVORY

Scones

LADEN WITH CHEESES, HERBS, MEATS, AND
VEGETABLES, THESE TASTY SCONES SERVE AS
A WELCOME DEPARTURE FROM THE TYPICAL
SWEET FARE THAT TEATIME BESTOWS.

Country Ham Scones
Makes 25

These hearty treats combine just five ingredients, featuring country ham as the star, to produce a scone that is truly a crowd-pleaser for all ages and tastes.

2 cups self-rising flour*
1 teaspoon cracked black pepper**
4 tablespoons cold unsalted butter, cubed
½ cup finely chopped cooked country ham
1 cup plus 1 tablespoon cold heavy whipping cream, divided

• Preheat oven to 450°. Line a rimmed baking sheet with parchment paper.
• In a large bowl, whisk together flour and pepper. Using a pastry blender or 2 forks, cut butter into flour mixture until it resembles coarse crumbs. Stir in ham.
• Add 1 cup cream to flour mixture, stirring until a shaggy dough begins to form. Working gently, bring mixture together in bowl with hands until a dough forms. (If dough won't come together, add more cream, 1 tablespoon at a time, until it does. Dough should be somewhat firm.)
• Turn out dough onto a lightly floured surface, and knead gently until smooth by patting dough and folding it in half 3 to 4 times. Using a rolling pin, roll out dough to a 1-inch thickness. Using a 1½-inch square cutter dipped in flour, cut 25 scones from dough without twisting cutter, rerolling scraps as necessary. Place scones 2 inches apart on prepared baking sheet.
• Brush tops of scones lightly with remaining 1 tablespoon cream.
• Bake until edges of scones are golden brown and a wooden pick inserted in the centers comes out clean, 7 to 8 minutes.

*We used White Lily.
**To crack peppercorns, place them in a heavy-duty resealable plastic bag and tap with a rolling pin or meat mallet to crush. If using already-ground black pepper, reduce amount to ½ teaspoon.

RECOMMENDED CONDIMENTS:
Clotted cream | Pepper jelly

Bacon-Spelt Scones
Makes 10

If a recipe includes bacon as an ingredient, it is usually a sign that it's going to be tasty. It's certainly no different with this remarkable scone, and a generous slather of our homemade Maple Butter takes this popular bake to the next level.

2 cups spelt flour*
1 tablespoon granulated sugar
2 teaspoons baking powder
½ teaspoon fine sea salt
¼ teaspoon ground black pepper
¼ cup unsalted butter, frozen
⅓ cup chopped crisp-cooked bacon
½ cup plus 2 tablespoons cold heavy whipping cream
¼ cup plus 1 tablespoon cold whole milk, divided

• Preheat oven to 350°. Line a rimmed baking sheet with parchment paper.
• In a large bowl, whisk together flour, sugar, baking powder, salt, and pepper. Using a coarse grater, grate frozen butter into flour mixture. Stir until grated butter is coated and evenly distributed. Stir in bacon.

• In a small bowl, stir together cream and ¼ cup milk. Add to flour mixture, stirring until a shaggy dough begins to form. Working gently, bring mixture together in bowl with hands until a dough forms. (If dough won't come together, add more cream, 1 tablespoon at a time, until it does. Dough should be firm.)
• Turn out dough onto a lightly floured surface (spelt flour), and knead gently until smooth by patting dough and folding it in half 4 to 5 times. Using a rolling pin, roll out dough to a ¾-inch thickness. Using a 2¼-inch fluted round cutter dipped in flour, cut 10 scones from dough without twisting cutter, rerolling scraps as necessary. Place scones 2 inches apart on prepared baking sheet.
• Brush tops of scones with remaining 1 tablespoon milk.
• Bake until edges of scones are golden brown and a wooden pick inserted in the centers comes out clean, approximately 20 minutes.

We used Bob's Red Mill Spelt Flour.

RECOMMENDED CONDIMENT:
Maple Butter (recipe on page 125)

Chocolate-Feta Scones
Makes 15

Chocolate and cheese might seem like an odd flavor pairing to some, but trust us, the deliciousness that results in the mingling of bittersweet chocolate and tangy feta in this scone is out of this world.

2 cups all-purpose flour
1 tablespoon granulated sugar
2 teaspoons baking powder
½ teaspoon fine sea salt
½ teaspoon freshly ground black pepper
4 tablespoons cold salted butter, cubed
1 cup bittersweet chocolate chips
1 (8-ounce) package feta cheese, coarsely chopped
1 cup plus 1 tablespoon cold heavy whipping cream,
  divided

• Preheat oven to 350°. Line a rimmed baking sheet with parchment paper.
• In a large bowl, whisk together flour, sugar, baking powder, salt, and pepper. Using a pastry blender or 2 forks, cut butter into flour mixture until it resembles coarse crumbs. Stir in chocolate morsels and feta.
• Add 1 cup cream to flour mixture, stirring until a shaggy dough begins to form. Working gently, bring mixture together in bowl with hands until a dough forms. (If dough won't come together, add more cream, 1 table-spoon at a time, until it does. Dough should be firm.)
• Turn out dough onto a lightly floured surface, and knead gently until smooth by patting dough and folding it in half 4 to 5 times. Using a rolling pin, roll out dough to a ¾-inch thickness. Using a 2¼-inch round cutter dipped in flour, cut 15 scones from dough without twist-ing cutter, rerolling scraps as necessary. Place scones 2 inches apart on prepared baking sheet.
• Brush tops of scones with remaining 1 tablespoon cream.
• Bake until edges of scones are golden brown and a wooden pick inserted in the centers comes out clean, approximately 20 minutes. Serve warm.

RECOMMENDED CONDIMENT:
Raspberry jam

"Everything" Scones
Makes 12

These tall scones mimic the delicious flavors that are found in the breakfast staple, the beloved Everything Bagel. Poppy seeds, sesame seeds, garlic, and minced onion are sprinkled on top to season these tantalizing scones that utilize bread flour and just a touch of light brown sugar in the dough.

3 cups bread flour
1 tablespoon light brown sugar
1 tablespoon baking powder
½ teaspoon fine sea salt
5 tablespoons cold unsalted butter, cubed
1¾ cups cold heavy whipping cream
1 egg white
1 tablespoon water
1 teaspoon poppy seeds
1 teaspoon sesame seeds
½ teaspoon dried garlic flakes
½ teaspoon dried minced onion
½ teaspoon coarse salt

• Preheat oven to 350°. Line a rimmed baking sheet with parchment paper.
• In a large bowl, whisk together flour, brown sugar, baking powder, and salt. Using a pastry blender or 2 forks, cut butter into flour mixture until it resembles coarse crumbs.
• Add cream to flour mixture, stirring until a shaggy dough begins to form. Working gently, bring mixture together in bowl with hands until a dough forms. (If dough won't come together, add more cream, 1 table-spoon at a time, until it does. Dough should be firm.)
• Turn out dough onto a lightly floured surface, and knead gently until smooth by patting dough and folding it in half 5 to 7 times. Using a rolling pin, roll out dough to a 1-inch thickness. Using a 2½-inch round cutter dipped in flour, cut 12 scones from dough without twist-ing cutter, rerolling scraps as necessary. Place scones 2 inches apart on prepared baking sheet.
• In a small bowl, whisk together egg white and 1 table-spoon water to make an egg wash. Brush tops of scones with egg wash.
• In another small bowl, stir together poppy seeds, sesame seeds, garlic flakes, onion, and coarse salt. Sprinkle evenly over tops of scones.

• Bake until edges of scones are golden brown and a wooden pick inserted in the centers comes out clean, 20 to 22 minutes. Serve warm.

RECOMMENDED CONDIMENTS:
Clotted cream | Orange marmalade

Corn, Goat Cheese & Chive Scones
Makes 13

Fresh corn, crumbled goat cheese, and chopped chives become a powerful trio in this appetizing bake that is a welcome change from the typical sweet scone. If chives don't strike your fancy, substitute scallions in their place for a similar taste and look, or you can omit them completely.

2 cups all-purpose flour
2 teaspoons baking powder
½ teaspoon fine sea salt
⅛ teaspoon ground black pepper
4 tablespoons cold salted butter, cubed
½ cup fresh corn kernels
½ cup crumbled goat cheese
1 tablespoon chopped fresh chives
¾ cup plus 3 tablespoons cold heavy whipping cream,
  divided

• Preheat oven to 350°. Line a rimmed baking sheet with parchment paper.
• In a large bowl, whisk together flour, baking powder, salt, and pepper. Using a pastry blender or 2 forks, cut butter into flour mixture until it resembles coarse crumbs. Stir in corn, goat cheese, and chives.
• Add ¾ cup plus 2 tablespoons cream to flour mixture, stirring until a shaggy dough begins to form. Working gently, bring mixture together in bowl with hands until a dough forms. (If dough won't come together, add more cream, 1 tablespoon at a time, until it does. Dough should be firm.)
• Turn out dough onto a lightly floured surface, and knead gently until smooth by patting dough and folding it in half 4 to 5 times. Using a rolling pin, roll out dough to a ¾-inch thickness. Using a 2-inch square cutter dipped in flour, cut 13 scones from dough without twisting cutter, rerolling scraps as necessary. Place scones 2 inches apart on prepared baking sheet.
• Brush tops of scones with remaining 1 tablespoon cream.
• Bake until edges of scones are golden brown and a wooden pick inserted in the centers comes out clean, approximately 20 minutes. Serve warm.

RECOMMENDED CONDIMENT:
Butter (salted or unsalted)

Onion–Poppy Seed Scones
Makes 13

This delicious scone, with an unusual flavor profile for afternoon tea, is laden with bits of caramelized sweet onion and studded with poppy seeds to create a wonderfully unique option to pair with tea.

2 teaspoons unsalted butter
2 teaspoons olive oil
1 cup sliced sweet onion
2 cups all-purpose flour
2 teaspoons granulated sugar
1½ teaspoons baking soda
1 teaspoon cream of tartar
½ teaspoon fine sea salt
4 tablespoons cold salted butter, cubed
3 teaspoons poppy seeds, divided
¾ cup cold whole buttermilk
1 large egg, beaten
1 teaspoon water
Garnish: grape halves

• Preheat oven to 425°. Line a rimmed baking sheet with parchment paper.
• In a small skillet, heat together unsalted butter and olive oil over medium heat until butter melts. Add onion, and cook, stirring occasionally, until onion is soft and very lightly browned, approximately 10 minutes. (Reduce heat if onion begins to brown too quickly.) Let onion cool, then finely chop.
• In a large bowl, whisk together flour, sugar, baking soda, cream of tartar, and salt. Using a pastry blender or 2 forks, cut salted butter into flour mixture until it resembles coarse crumbs. Stir in caramelized onion and 1 teaspoon poppy seeds.
• Add buttermilk to flour mixture, stirring until a soft dough forms.
• Turn out dough onto a lightly floured surface, and knead gently until smooth by patting dough and folding it in half 3 to 4 times. Using a rolling pin, roll out dough to a ¾-inch thickness. Using a 2-inch fluted round cutter dipped in flour, cut 13 scones from dough without twisting cutter, rerolling scraps as necessary. Place scones 2 inches apart on prepared baking sheet.
• In a small bowl, whisk together egg and 1 teaspoon water to make an egg wash. Brush tops of scones

with egg wash. Sprinkle with remaining 2 teaspoons poppy seeds.
• Bake until edges of scones are golden brown and a wooden pick inserted in the centers comes out clean, approximately 9 minutes. Serve warm.
• Garnish individual servings with grape halves, if desired.

RECOMMENDED CONDIMENTS:
Clotted cream | Orange marmalade

Walnut & Olive Whole-Wheat Scones

Makes 11

Prepared with whole-wheat and all-purpose flours, this yummy, hearty scone is filled with toasted walnuts and kalamata olives to provide a great savory alternative for teatime or for a light snack.

1½ cups whole-wheat flour
½ cup all-purpose flour
1 tablespoon granulated sugar
2¼ teaspoons baking powder
½ teaspoon fine sea salt
4 tablespoons cold salted butter, cubed
⅓ cup chopped toasted walnuts
¼ cup chopped kalamata olives
1 cup plus 2 tablespoons cold heavy whipping cream, divided

- Preheat oven to 350°. Line a rimmed baking sheet with parchment paper.
- In a large bowl, whisk together whole-wheat flour, all-purpose flour, sugar, baking powder, and salt. Using a pastry blender or 2 forks, cut butter into flour mixture until it resembles coarse crumbs. Stir in walnuts and olives until coated with flour.
- Add 1 cup plus 1 tablespoon cream to flour mixture, stirring until a dry, shaggy dough begins to form. Working gently, bring mixture together in bowl with hands until a dough forms. (If dough won't come together, add more cream, 1 tablespoon at a time, until it does. Dough should be firm.)
- Turn out dough onto a lightly floured surface, and knead gently until smooth by patting dough and folding it in half 4 to 5 times. Using a rolling pin, roll out dough to a ¾-inch thickness. Using a 2¼-inch round cutter dipped in flour, cut 11 scones from dough without twisting cutter, rerolling scraps as necessary. Place scones 2 inches apart on prepared baking sheet.
- Brush tops of scones with remaining 1 tablespoon cream.
- Bake scones until edges are golden brown, approximately 20 minutes. Serve warm.

RECOMMENDED CONDIMENT:
Clotted cream

Brie & Olive Scones
Makes 14

Creamy Brie cheese tones down the bitterness of Picholine olives in this brilliant and satisfying bake that will draw rave reviews at your next afternoon tea.

2¼ cups all-purpose flour
1 tablespoon granulated sugar
2½ teaspoons baking powder
½ teaspoon fine sea salt
¼ teaspoon ground black pepper
¼ cup cold unsalted butter, cubed
½ cup coarsely chopped Picholine olives
4 ounces Brie cheese, cut into ¼-inch cubes
    (approximately ¾ cup)
½ cup plus 3 tablespoons cold heavy whipping cream,
    divided
1 large egg

- Preheat oven to 375°. Line a rimmed baking sheet with parchment paper.
- In a large bowl, whisk together flour, sugar, baking powder, salt, and pepper. Using a pastry blender or 2 forks, cut in butter until it resembles coarse crumbs. Stir in olives and cheese until coated with flour.
- In a small bowl, whisk together ½ cup plus 2 tablespoons cream and egg. Add to flour mixture, stirring until a shaggy dough begins to form. Working gently, bring mixture together in bowl with hands until a dough forms. (If dough won't come together, add more cream, 1 tablespoon at a time, until it does. Dough should be somewhat firm.)
- Turn out dough onto a lightly floured surface, and knead gently until smooth by patting dough and folding it in half 8 to 10 times. Using a rolling pin, roll out dough to a ¾-inch thickness. Using a 2½-inch round cutter dipped in flour, cut 14 scones from dough without twisting cutter, rerolling scraps as necessary. Place scones 2 inches apart on prepared baking sheet.
- Brush tops of scones with remaining 1 tablespoon cream.
- Bake until scones are golden brown, approximately 23 minutes. Serve warm.

RECOMMENDED CONDIMENT:
Honey Butter (recipe on page 125)

Kalamata Olive–Rosemary Scones
Makes approximately 15

The woodsy notes of rosemary mingle with salty olives in this divine teatime delight that is sure to please a crowd.

2 cups bread flour
1 tablespoon finely chopped fresh rosemary
2 teaspoons baking powder
½ teaspoon fine sea salt
4 tablespoons cold salted butter, cubed
3 tablespoons finely chopped Kalamata olives
1¼ cups cold heavy whipping cream, divided
Garnish: fresh rosemary sprigs

• Preheat oven to 350°. Line a rimmed baking sheet with parchment paper.
• In a large bowl, whisk together flour, rosemary, baking powder, and salt. Using a pastry blender or 2 forks, cut butter into flour mixture until it resembles coarse crumbs. Stir in olives.
• Reserving 1 tablespoon cream, add remaining 1 cup plus 3 tablespoons cream to flour mixture, stirring until a shaggy dough begins to form. Working gently, bring mixture together in bowl with hands until a dough forms. (If dough won't come together, add more cream, 1 tablespoon at a time, until it does. Dough should be firm.)
• Turn out dough onto a lightly floured surface, and knead gently until smooth by patting dough and folding it in half 3 to 5 times. Using a rolling pin, roll out dough to a ½-inch thickness. Using a 2-inch square cutter dipped in flour, cut as many scones as possible from dough without twisting cutter, rerolling scraps as necessary. Place scones 2 inches apart on prepared baking sheet.
• Brush tops of scones with reserved 1 tablespoon cream.
• Bake until edges of scones are golden brown and a wooden pick inserted in the centers comes out clean, approximately 20 minutes. Serve warm.
• Garnish with rosemary sprigs, if desired.

RECOMMENDED CONDIMENT:
Black Pepper Butter Rosettes (recipe on page 126)

White Cheddar–Rosemary Scones
Makes 10

Sharp Cheddar cheese and fresh rosemary pair together beautifully in this lovely bake. This recipe was developed specifically for winter gatherings but can be enjoyed year-round and elevated by toppings such as fig preserves.

2½ cups all-purpose flour
1 tablespoon baking powder
¾ teaspoon fine sea salt
4 tablespoons cold unsalted butter, cubed
1 cup coarsely shredded sharp white Cheddar cheese
2 teaspoons minced fresh rosemary
1¼ cups cold heavy whipping cream, divided

• Preheat oven to 375°. Line a rimmed baking sheet with parchment paper.
• In a large bowl, whisk together flour, baking powder, and salt. Using a pastry blender or 2 forks, cut in butter until it resembles coarse crumbs. Stir in cheese and rosemary.
• Add 1 cup plus 3 tablespoons cream to flour mixture, stirring until a shaggy dough begins to form. Working gently, bring mixture together in bowl with hands until a dough forms. (If dough won't come together, add more cream, 1 tablespoon at a time, until it does. Dough should be firm.)
• Turn out dough onto a lightly floured surface, and knead gently until smooth by patting dough and folding it in half 4 to 5 times. Using a rolling pin, roll out dough to a ¾-inch thickness. Using a 2¼-inch round cutter dipped in flour, cut 10 scones from dough without twisting cutter, rerolling scraps as necessary. Place scones 2 inches apart on prepared baking sheet.
• Brush tops of scones with remaining 1 tablespoon cream.
• Bake until edges of scones are golden brown and a wooden pick inserted in the centers comes out clean, approximately 20 minutes. Serve warm.

RECOMMENDED CONDIMENT:
Fig preserves

New Zealand Cheddar Scones
Makes approximately 10

New Zealand is renowned for its dairy products. These scones, made with self-rising flour, incorporate Cheddar cheese from the island nation for a remarkable treat.

2½ cups self-rising flour
1½ teaspoons granulated sugar
¼ teaspoon fine sea salt
3 tablespoons cold unsalted butter, cubed
½ cup shredded New Zealand Cheddar cheese
¾ cup plus 1 tablespoon cold heavy whipping cream, divided

• Preheat oven to 400°. Line a rimmed baking sheet with parchment paper.
• In a medium bowl, whisk together flour, sugar, and salt. Using a pastry blender or 2 forks, cut butter into flour mixture until it resembles coarse crumbs. Stir in cheese.
• Gradually add ¾ cup cream to flour mixture, stirring until a shaggy dough begins to form. Working gently, bring mixture together in bowl with hands until a dough forms. (If dough won't come together, add more cream, 1 tablespoon at a time, until it does. Dough should be somewhat firm.)
• Turn out dough onto a lightly floured surface, and knead gently until smooth by patting dough and folding it in half 4 to 5 times. Using a rolling pin, roll out dough to a ¾-inch thickness. Using a sharp knife, cut dough into four equal pieces. Stack pieces on top of each other. Using a rolling pin, roll out dough to a ¾-inch thickness. Using a 2-inch round cutter dipped in flour, cut 10 scones from dough without twisting cutter, rerolling scraps once. Place scones on prepared baking sheet.
• Brush tops of scones with remaining 1 tablespoon cream.
• Bake until scones are golden brown, 10 to 12 minutes. Let cool on baking sheet for 5 minutes. Serve warm.

RECOMMENDED CONDIMENT:
Golden Kiwi Jam (recipe on page 127)

Apple-Cheddar Scones
Makes 13 to 14

These perfectly plump scones are laden with extra-sharp white Cheddar cheese and Gala apples for the ideal balance of savory and sweet. To enhance the sweet taste of apple, consider adding a dollop of clotted cream and orange marmalade to top your scone.

3 cups all-purpose flour
2 tablespoons granulated sugar
4 teaspoons baking powder
½ teaspoon fine sea salt
½ cup cold unsalted butter, cubed
¾ cup shredded extra-sharp white Cheddar cheese
½ cup diced unpeeled Gala apples
1 cup plus 5 tablespoons cold heavy whipping cream, divided

• Preheat oven to 375°. Line a rimmed baking sheet with parchment paper.
• In a large bowl, whisk together flour, sugar, baking powder, and salt. Using a pastry blender or 2 forks, cut butter into flour mixture until it resembles coarse crumbs. Stir in cheese and apples.
• Add 1 cup plus 3 tablespoons cream to flour mixture, stirring until a dry, shaggy dough begins to form. Working gently, bring mixture together in bowl with hands until a dough forms. (If dough won't come together, add more cream, 1 tablespoon at a time, until it does. Dough should be firm.)
• Turn out dough onto a lightly floured surface, and knead gently until smooth by patting dough and folding it in half 4 to 5 times. Using a rolling pin, roll out dough to a ¾-inch thickness. Using a 2¼-inch round cutter dipped in flour, cut as many scones as possible from dough without twisting cutter, rerolling scraps once. Place scones 2 inches apart on prepared baking sheet.
• Brush tops of scones with remaining 2 tablespoons cream.
• Bake until edges of scones are golden brown and a wooden pick inserted in the centers comes out clean, 20 to 25 minutes. Serve warm.

RECOMMENDED CONDIMENTS:
Clotted cream | Orange marmalade

Rosemary-Parmesan Scones
Makes 11

Finely chopped fresh rosemary and grated Parmesan cheese combine beautifully in this herbaceous scone that can be cut using a square cutter, as pictured, or a round one for a more traditional look.

2 cups all-purpose flour
2 teaspoons baking powder
1½ teaspoons finely chopped fresh rosemary
½ teaspoon fine sea salt
¼ teaspoon ground black pepper
4 tablespoons cold salted butter, cubed
1½ cups finely grated Parmesan cheese
1 cup plus 1 tablespoon cold heavy whipping cream,
   divided
Garnish: freshly ground black pepper

• Preheat oven to 350°. Line a rimmed baking sheet with parchment paper.
• In a large bowl, whisk together flour, baking powder, rosemary, salt, and pepper. Using a pastry blender or 2 forks, cut butter into flour mixture until it resembles coarse crumbs. Stir in cheese.
• Add 1 cup cream, stirring until a shaggy dough begins to form. Working gently, bring mixture together in bowl with hands until a dough forms. (If dough won't come together, add more cream, 1 tablespoon at a time, until it does. Dough should be firm.)
• Turn out dough onto a lightly floured surface, and knead gently until smooth by patting dough and folding it in half 4 to 5 times. Using a rolling pin, roll out dough to a ¾-inch thickness. Using a 2-inch square cutter dipped in flour, cut 11 scones from dough without twisting cutter, rerolling scraps as necessary. Place scones 2 inches apart on prepared baking sheet.
• Brush tops of scones with remaining 1 tablespoon cream. Garnish scones with a sprinkle of freshly ground pepper, if desired.
• Bake until edges of scones are golden brown and a wooden pick inserted in the centers comes out clean, approximately 20 minutes. Serve warm.

RECOMMENDED CONDIMENT:
Clotted cream

Parmesan-Sage Scones
Makes 12

Teatime guests will enjoy these charmingly round, cheesy, and herby scones that are brimming with bold flavor. For a seasonally appropriate variation in the fall, serve them with pumpkin butter, either homemade or store-bought.

2 cups all-purpose flour
1 tablespoon granulated sugar
2 teaspoons baking powder
2 teaspoons ground sage
1½ teaspoons fresh thyme
½ teaspoon fine sea salt
4 tablespoons cold salted butter, cubed
1 cup grated Parmesan cheese
1 cup plus 1 tablespoon heavy whipping cream, divided

• Preheat oven to 350°. Line a rimmed baking sheet with parchment paper.
• In a large bowl, whisk together flour, sugar, baking powder, sage, thyme, and salt. Using a pastry blender or 2 forks, cut butter into flour mixture until it resembles coarse crumbs. Stir in cheese.
• Add ¾ cup plus 3 tablespoons cream to flour mixture, stirring until a shaggy dough begins to form. Working gently, bring mixture together in bowl with hands until a dough forms. (If dough won't come together, add more cream, 1 tablespoon at a time, until it does. Dough should be quite firm.)
• Turn out dough onto a lightly floured surface, and knead gently until smooth by patting dough and folding it in half 4 to 5 times. Using a rolling pin, roll out dough to a ¾-inch thickness. Using a 2¼-inch round cutter dipped in flour, cut 12 scones from dough without twisting cutter, rerolling scraps as necessary. Place scones 2 inches apart on prepared baking sheet.
• Brush tops of scones with remaining 2 tablespoons cream.
• Bake until edges of scones are golden brown and a wooden pick inserted in the centers comes out clean, approximately 20 minutes. Serve warm.

RECOMMENDED CONDIMENT:
Pumpkin butter

Mini Dilled Scones
Makes 20

Petite and well-suited for a spring garden party, these bite-size and crave-worthy delights are made with black pepper, fresh dill, and cottage cheese—a surprising ingredient that adds extra moisture and texture to the scone.

1½ cups all-purpose flour
1½ teaspoons baking powder
1 teaspoon granulated sugar
1 teaspoon dried minced onion
¼ teaspoon fine sea salt

⅛ teaspoon ground black pepper
1 tablespoon finely chopped fresh dill*
4 tablespoons cold salted butter, cubed
½ cup plus 1 tablespoon cold heavy whipping cream, divided
⅓ cup small-curd cottage cheese

• Preheat oven to 350°. Line a rimmed baking sheet with parchment paper.
• In a large bowl, whisk together flour, baking powder, sugar, dried onion, salt, and pepper. Whisk in dill. Using a pastry blender or 2 forks, cut butter into flour mixture until it resembles coarse crumbs.

- In a small bowl, stir together ½ cup cream and cottage cheese. Add to flour mixture, stirring until a shaggy dough begins to form. Working gently, bring mixture together in bowl with hands until a dough forms. (If dough won't come together, add more cream, 1 tablespoon at a time, until it does. Dough should be somewhat firm.)
- Turn out dough onto a lightly floured surface, and knead gently until smooth by patting dough and folding it in half 3 to 4 times. Using a rolling pin, roll out dough to a ½-inch thickness. Using a 1½-inch square cutter dipped in flour, cut 20 scones from dough without twisting cutter, rerolling scraps as necessary. Place scones 2 inches apart on prepared baking sheet.
- Brush tops of scones with remaining 1 tablespoon cream.
- Bake until edges of scones are golden brown, approximately 18 minutes. Serve warm or at room temperature.

To easily chop dill very finely, place in a small bowl and snip with kitchen scissors.

RECOMMENDED CONDIMENT:
Clotted cream

Dill-Havarti Wedge Scones
Makes 12

The thick doughy layers of these lovely triangles boast the vibrant and pleasant taste of dill Havarti cheese.

2½ cups all-purpose flour
2½ teaspoons baking powder
½ teaspoon fine sea salt
¼ teaspoon ground black pepper
6 tablespoons cold unsalted butter, cubed
1½ cups shredded dill Havarti cheese
1¼ cups cold heavy whipping cream, divided
Garnish: freshly ground black pepper

- Preheat oven to 350°. Line a rimmed baking sheet with parchment paper.
- In a large bowl, whisk together flour, baking powder, salt, and pepper. Using a pastry blender or 2 forks, cut butter into flour mixture until it resembles coarse crumbs. Stir in cheese.

- Add 1 cup plus 3 tablespoons cream to flour mixture, stirring until a shaggy dough begins to form. Working gently, bring mixture together in bowl with hands until a dough forms. (If dough won't come together, add more cream, 1 tablespoon at a time, until it does. Dough should be firm.)
- Turn out dough onto a lightly floured surface, and knead gently until smooth by patting dough and folding it in half 4 to 5 times. Divide dough into 2 equal portions. Using a rolling pin, roll each portion to a ¾-inch-thick disk. Using a long sharp knife and pressing downward, cut each disk into 6 wedge scones. Place scones 2 inches apart on prepared baking sheet.
- Brush tops of scones with remaining 1 tablespoon cream. Garnish scones with a dusting of freshly ground black pepper, if desired.
- Bake until edges of scones are golden brown and a wooden pick inserted in the centers comes out clean, approximately 20 minutes. Serve warm.

RECOMMENDED CONDIMENT:
Whipped butter

"Blue Suede" Scones
Makes 11

A tribute to the "King of Rock and Roll" and Elvis Presley's hit song "Blue Suede Shoes," these scones are packed with fruity flavor from blueberries and delightful zing from blue cheese crumbles to create a well-balanced treat that might cause a standing ovation upon consumption.

2 cups all-purpose flour
1 tablespoon granulated sugar
2 teaspoons baking powder
½ teaspoon fine sea salt
⅛ teaspoon ground black pepper
4 tablespoons cold unsalted butter, cubed
½ cup dried blueberries
⅓ cup blue cheese crumbles
1 cup plus 1 tablespoon cold heavy whipping cream, divided

• Preheat oven to 350°. Line a rimmed baking sheet with parchment paper.
• In a large bowl, whisk together flour, sugar, baking powder, salt, and pepper. Using a pastry blender or 2 forks, cut butter into flour mixture until it resembles coarse crumbs. Stir in blueberries and blue cheese.
• Add 1 cup cream to flour mixture, stirring until a shaggy dough begins to form. Working gently, bring mixture together in bowl with hands until a dough forms. (If dough won't come together, add more cream, 1 tablespoon at a time, until it does. Dough should be firm.)
• Turn out dough onto a lightly floured surface, and knead gently until smooth by patting dough and folding it in half 4 to 5 times. Using a rolling pin, roll out dough to a ¾-inch thickness. Using a 2¼-inch square cutter dipped in flour, cut 11 scones from dough without twisting cutter, rerolling scraps as necessary. Place scones 2 inches apart on prepared baking sheet.
• Brush tops of scones with remaining 1 tablespoon cream.
• Bake until edges of scones are golden brown and a wooden pick inserted in the centers comes out clean, 17 to 20 minutes. Serve warm or at room temperature.

RECOMMENDED CONDIMENT:
Clotted cream

Date, Chive & Parmesan Scones
Makes approximately 10

Mostly savory thanks to fresh chives and Parmesan but sweetened slightly with the addition of dates, this complex scone is bursting with marvelous flavor in every crumb.

3 cups all-purpose flour
1 tablespoon granulated sugar
1 tablespoon baking powder
½ teaspoon fine sea salt
8 tablespoons cold unsalted butter, cubed
½ cup diced pitted dates*
½ cup very finely freshly grated Parmigiano-Reggiano
   cheese**
2 tablespoons chopped fresh chives
1¼ cups plus 1 tablespoon cold heavy whipping cream,
   divided

• Preheat oven to 375°. Line a rimmed baking sheet with parchment paper.
• In a large bowl, whisk together flour, sugar, baking powder, and salt. Using a pastry blender or 2 forks, cut butter into flour mixture until it resembles coarse crumbs. Add dates, cheese, and chives, tossing to combine.
• Add 1¼ cups cream to flour mixture, stirring until a shaggy dough begins to form. Working gently, bring mixture together in bowl with hands until a dough forms. (If dough won't come together, add more cream, 1 tablespoon at a time, until it does. Dough should be somewhat firm.)
• Turn out dough onto a lightly floured surface, and knead gently until smooth by patting dough and folding it in half 3 to 4 times. Using a rolling pin, roll out dough to a ¾-inch thickness. Fold dough into thirds (like an envelope). Roll dough again to a ¾-inch thickness. Using a 2¼-inch round cutter dipped in flour, cut as many scones as possible from dough without twisting cutter, rerolling scraps once. Place scones 1 inch apart on prepared baking sheet. Freeze for 10 minutes.
• Brush tops of scones with remaining 1 tablespoon cream.
• Bake until scones are golden brown and a wooden pick inserted in the centers comes out clean, approximately 17 minutes. Let cool on baking sheet for 5 minutes. Serve warm or at room temperature.

*We used Sunsweet Pitted Dates and sprinkled dates with a little flour to make less sticky and easier to chop.
**We used a Microplane grater, which makes the grated cheese light and fluffy. To measure, loosely pack in measuring cup.

RECOMMENDED CONDIMENT:
Clotted cream

ALMOND
SUGAR-FREE SCONES,
page 110

ALLERGY-FRIENDLY

Scones

WHETHER YOU HAVE DIETARY RESTRICTIONS
OR ARE SIMPLY TRYING TO EAT HEALTHIER,
THESE GLUTEN-FREE, VEGAN-FRIENDLY, AND
LOW-CARB BAKES WILL DELIGHT.

• Add 1⅓ cups cream to flour mixture, stirring until a shaggy dough begins to form. Working gently, bring mixture together in bowl with hands until a dough forms. (If dough won't come together, add more cream, 1 tablespoon at a time, until it does. Dough should be somewhat firm.)
• Turn out dough onto a lightly floured* surface, and knead gently until smooth by patting dough and folding it in half 4 to 5 times. Using a rolling pin, roll out dough to a 1-inch thickness. Using a 2-inch fluted round cutter dipped in flour*, cut 12 scones from dough without twisting cutter, rerolling scraps as necessary. Place scones 2 inches apart on prepared baking sheet.
• Brush tops of scones with remaining 1 tablespoon cream.
• Bake until edges of scones are golden brown and a wooden pick inserted in the centers comes out clean, approximately 10 minutes. Serve warm.

*We had good results with Pamela's Artisan Flour Blend.

RECOMMENDED CONDIMENTS:
Clotted cream | Lemon curd | Orange marmalade

Cream Gluten-free Scones
Makes 12

Enjoy this gluten-free version of a traditional cream scone with classic English condiments such as clotted cream, lemon curd, and orange marmalade.

2 cups gluten-free all-purpose flour blend*
2 tablespoons granulated sugar
2½ teaspoons baking powder
½ teaspoon fine sea salt
4 tablespoons cold salted butter, cubed
1⅓ cups plus 1 tablespoon cold heavy whipping cream, divided

• Preheat oven to 400°. Line a rimmed baking sheet with parchment paper.
• In a large bowl, whisk together flour, sugar, baking powder, and salt. Using a pastry blender or 2 forks, cut butter into flour mixture until it resembles coarse crumbs.

Toasted Pecan & Coconut Dairy-free Scones
Makes 20

Even teatime guests who don't have dietary sensitivities will thoroughly enjoy these flavorful gluten-free scones that are also vegan. Toasted pecans and three different types of coconut—oil, milk, and grated—add irresistible taste to this beautiful bake.

6 tablespoons coconut oil
2 cups gluten-free all-purpose flour blend*
¼ cup granulated sugar
1 tablespoon firmly packed dark brown sugar
1 tablespoon baking powder
½ teaspoon fine sea salt
¼ cup unsweetened grated coconut, toasted and cooled
¼ cup chopped pecans, toasted and cooled
1 cup plus 1 tablespoon cold organic coconut milk, divided
½ teaspoon vanilla extract

- Line a rimmed baking sheet with parchment paper.
- Place coconut oil in a shallow bowl. Refrigerate until coconut oil begins to solidify, 5 to 10 minutes. Using a fork, score coconut oil deeply to create a fine grid pattern. Refrigerate until firm, 15 to 20 minutes more. Using hands, quickly break coconut oil into very small pieces.
- In a large bowl, whisk together flour, granulated sugar, brown sugar, baking powder, and salt. Using a pastry blender or 2 forks, cut in cold coconut oil until it resembles coarse crumbs. (If coconut oil is too hard or too soft, it will be difficult to work with. If too hard, let sit at room temperature for a few minutes. If too soft, refrigerate for a few minutes.) Stir in grated coconut and pecans.
- In a small bowl, stir together 1 cup coconut milk and vanilla extract. Add coconut milk mixture to flour mixture, stirring until a dough begins to form. Working gently and quickly, bring mixture together in bowl with hands until a dough forms. (If dough won't come together, add more coconut milk, 1 tablespoon at a time, until it does. Dough should be somewhat firm.)
- Turn out dough onto a lightly floured* surface, and knead gently and quickly until smooth by patting dough and folding it in half 4 to 5 times. Using a rolling pin, roll out dough to a ¾-inch thickness. Using a 1¾-inch fluted round cutter dipped in flour*, cut 20 scones from dough without twisting cutter, rerolling scraps as necessary. Place scones 2 inches apart on prepared baking sheet. Freeze for at least 30 minutes†.
- Preheat oven to 400°.
- Brush tops of frozen scones with remaining 1 tablespoon coconut milk.
- Bake until edges of scones are golden brown and a wooden pick inserted in the centers comes out clean, 15 to 20 minutes. Serve warm.

*Gluten-free flour blends such as Bob's Red Mill Gluten Free 1-to-1 Baking Flour, Cup4Cup Gluten Free Multipurpose Flour, or King Arthur Gluten Free Measure for Measure Flour are best for scones.

†At this point, scones can be frozen completely and then transferred to an airtight freezer bag for longer storage, up to 3 months. Just before serving, place desired number of frozen scones on parchment paper–lined rimmed baking sheets and bake without thawing, according to remaining recipe instructions and allowing a few extra minutes for proper browning and doneness.

RECOMMENDED CONDIMENT:
Strawberry preserves

Cherry-Matcha Gluten-free Scones
Makes 12

A cream scone delightfully flavored with culinary-grade Matcha (powdered Japanese green tea) and spiked with dried cherries is a lovely scone to serve for a Christmas tea and beyond.

2 cups gluten-free all-purpose flour blend*
⅓ cup plus 1 teaspoon granulated sugar, divided
2 tablespoons Matcha green tea powder
2 teaspoons baking powder
½ teaspoon fine sea salt
4 tablespoons cold unsalted butter, cubed
½ cup dried cherries
1¼ cups cold heavy whipping cream
¼ teaspoon vanilla extract
¼ teaspoon almond extract

• Preheat oven to 350°. Line a rimmed baking sheet with parchment paper.
• In a large bowl, whisk together flour, ⅓ cup sugar, Matcha, baking powder, and salt. Using a pastry blender or 2 forks, cut butter into flour mixture until it resembles coarse crumbs. Add cherries, tossing to combine.

• In a liquid-measuring cup, stir together cream, vanilla extract, and almond extract. Add to flour mixture, stirring until a shaggy dough begins to form. Working gently, bring mixture together in bowl with hands until a dough forms. (If dough won't come together, add more cream, 1 tablespoon at a time, until it does. Dough should be somewhat firm.)
• Turn out dough onto a lightly floured* surface, and knead gently until smooth by patting dough and folding it in half 3 to 5 times. Using a rolling pin, roll out dough to a 1-inch thickness. Using a 2¼-inch round cutter dipped in flour*, cut 12 scones from dough without twisting cutter, rerolling scraps as necessary. Place scones 2 inches apart on prepared baking sheet.
• Sprinkle tops of scones with remaining 1 teaspoon sugar.
• Bake until edges of scones are golden brown and a wooden pick inserted in the centers comes out clean. Serve warm or at room temperature.

We used Pillsbury Gluten Free All Purpose Flour.

RECOMMENDED CONDIMENTS:
Clotted cream | Lemon curd

Vanilla-Orange Earl Grey Gluten-free Scones

Makes 11

A hint of citrus and vanilla only adds to the divine flavor of these tea-laced scones, making them the perfect wintry treat when served warm from the oven. If a mortar and pestle are not available to grind the Earl Grey tea leaves, a small food processor will work well.

1 cup plus 2 tablespoons heavy whipping cream
3 tablespoons Earl Grey tea leaves, divided
1 vanilla bean pod
2 cups gluten-free all-purpose flour blend for baking*
⅓ cup granulated sugar
1 tablespoon fresh orange zest
2 teaspoons baking powder
½ teaspoon fine sea salt
6 tablespoons unsalted butter, frozen
1 large egg

• In a small saucepan, heat cream over medium-high heat to just below a simmer. Remove from heat. Add 2 tablespoons tea leaves, cover, and let steep for 10 minutes.
• Using a fine-mesh sieve, strain cream mixture into a bowl, discarding tea leaves. Cover bowl and refrigerate until very cold, approximately 6 hours.
• Preheat oven to 350°. Line a rimmed baking sheet with parchment paper.
• Using a mortar and pestle, grind remaining 1 tablespoon tea leaves until very fine.
• Using a sharp knife, split vanilla bean pod lengthwise, and reserve seeds, discarding pod.
• In a large bowl, whisk together flour, sugar, orange zest, baking powder, salt, and reserved vanilla bean seeds. Using a coarse grater, grate frozen butter into flour mixture. Stir until grated butter is coated and evenly distributed.
• Add egg to chilled cream, whisking to combine. Add cream mixture to flour mixture, stirring until a shaggy dough begins to form. Working gently, bring mixture together in bowl with hands until a dough forms. (If dough won't come together, add more cream, 1 tablespoon at a time, until it does. Dough should be somewhat firm.)
• Turn out dough onto a lightly floured* surface, and knead gently until smooth by patting dough and folding it in half 4 to 5 times. Using a rolling pin, roll out dough to a 1-inch thickness. Using a 2¼-inch fluted round

cutter dipped in flour*, cut 11 scones from dough without twisting cutter, rerolling scraps as necessary. Place scones 2 inches apart on prepared baking sheet.
• Bake until edges of scones are golden brown and a wooden pick inserted in the centers comes out clean, approximately 20 minutes. Serve warm.

For testing purposes, we used Pamela's Gluten-Free All-Purpose Flour Mix.

RECOMMENDED CONDIMENTS:
Faux Clotted Cream (recipe on page 122) | Lemon curd

Honey-Orange Gluten-free Scones
Makes 12

*Rich dark honey and bright notes of dried orange peel
fill this gluten-free scone with a delicate sweetness and
delectable flavor.*

2 cups gluten-free all-purpose flour blend
1 tablespoon dried Valencia orange peel*
2 teaspoons baking powder
½ teaspoon fine sea salt
⅛ teaspoon baking soda
6 tablespoons cold unsalted butter, cubed
¾ cup plus 1 tablespoon cold heavy whipping cream,
   divided
⅓ cup dark honey
¼ teaspoon vanilla extract

• Preheat oven to 350°. Line a rimmed baking sheet
with parchment paper.
• In a large bowl, whisk together flour, orange peel,
baking powder, salt, and baking soda. Using a pastry
blender or 2 forks, cut butter into flour mixture until
it resembles coarse crumbs.
• In a small bowl, stir together ¾ cup cream, honey,
and vanilla extract. Add to flour mixture, stirring until
a shaggy dough begins to form. Working gently, bring
mixture together in bowl with hands until a dough
forms. (If dough won't come together, add more cream,
1 tablespoon at a time, until it does. Dough should be
somewhat firm.)
• Turn out dough onto a lightly floured** surface, and
knead gently until smooth by patting dough and folding it in half 4 to 5 times. Using a rolling pin, roll dough
to a 1-inch thickness. Using a 2-inch fluted round cutter
dipped in flour**, cut 12 scones from dough without
twisting cutter, rerolling scraps as necessary. Place
scones 2 inches apart on prepared baking sheet.
• Brush tops of scones with remaining 1 tablespoon cream.
• Bake until edges of scones are golden brown and
a wooden pick inserted in the centers comes
out clean, 15 to 16 minutes. Serve warm.

We used McCormick Gourmet Dried Valencia Orange Peel.
**We used gluten-free all-purpose flour blend.*

RECOMMENDED CONDIMENT:
Clotted cream

Currant-Orange Gluten-free Scones
Makes 16 to 18

Dipped in warm butter and sprinkled with orange sugar, these sticky-sweet scones make an excellent first course or segue to the final course of afternoon tea.

2 cups gluten-free all-purpose flour blend
½ cup granulated sugar, divided
1 tablespoon baking powder
½ teaspoon fine sea salt
4 tablespoons cold unsalted butter, cubed
½ cup dried currants
2 tablespoons fresh orange zest, divided
¾ cup cold buttermilk
2 large eggs
3 tablespoons heavy whipping cream
4 tablespoons butter, melted

• Preheat oven to 425°. Line 2 rimmed baking sheets with parchment paper.
• In a large bowl, whisk together flour, ¼ cup sugar, baking powder, and salt. Using a pastry blender or 2 forks, cut butter into flour mixture until it resembles coarse crumbs. Stir in currants and 1 tablespoon orange zest.
• In a small bowl, combine remaining ¼ cup sugar and remaining 1 tablespoon orange zest. Using fingers, rub zest into sugar until well blended and sugar is orange. Set aside to use later for sprinkling.
• In another small bowl, whisk together buttermilk and eggs. Add to flour mixture, stirring until a shaggy dough begins to form. Working gently, bring mixture together in bowl with hands until a dough forms. (If dough won't come together, add more buttermilk, 1 tablespoon at a time, until it does. Dough should be somewhat firm.)
• Turn out dough onto a lightly floured* surface, and knead gently until smooth by patting dough and folding it in half 4 to 5 times. Using a rolling pin, roll out dough to a ½-inch thickness. Using a 2-inch round cutter dipped in flour*, cut as many scones as possible from dough without twisting cutter, rerolling scraps only once. Place scones 2 inches apart on prepared baking sheets.
• Brush tops of scones with cream.
• Bake until edges of scones are lightly golden brown and a wooden pick inserted in the centers comes out clean, approximately 10 minutes. Let cool slightly on wire racks.

• Dip tops of warm scones in melted butter, and sprinkle with orange sugar.

*We used gluten-free all-purpose flour blend.

RECOMMENDED CONDIMENTS:
Clotted cream | Lemon curd

Honeyed Lavender Gluten-free Scones

Makes 12 to 14

The luscious texture of these scones is largely due to the secret ingredient—cream cheese! Honey, which replaces the usual granulated sugar in the recipe, adds a perfect level of gentle sweetness, while culinary-grade lavender, which is pesticide-free, imparts a delightful floral fragrance and flavor, not to mention serving as a delicate garnish.

2 cups gluten-free all-purpose flour blend*
1 tablespoon baking power
1¼ teaspoons dried culinary lavender, divided
¼ teaspoon fine sea salt
4 tablespoons cold unsalted butter, cubed
2 ounces cold cream cheese, cubed
1 cup plus 1 tablespoon cold heavy whipping cream, divided
3 tablespoons plus ¼ teaspoon honey, divided
¼ teaspoon vanilla extract

• Line a rimmed baking sheet with parchment paper.
• In a large bowl, whisk together flour, baking powder, ¾ teaspoon lavender, and salt. Using a pastry blender or 2 forks, cut butter and cream cheese into flour mixture until they resemble coarse crumbs.

• In a small bowl, whisk together 1 cup cream, 3 tablespoons honey, and vanilla extract. Add cream mixture to flour mixture, stirring until a dough begins to form. Working gently, bring mixture together in bowl with hands until a dough forms.
• Turn out dough onto a lightly floured* surface, and knead gently until smooth by patting dough and folding it in half 3 to 4 times. Using a rolling pin, roll out dough to a ¾- to 1-inch thickness. Using a 1⅞-inch round cutter dipped in flour*, cut as many scones as possible from dough without twisting cutter, rerolling scraps no more than once. Place scones, evenly spaced, on prepared baking sheet. Freeze scones for at least 20 minutes†.
• Preheat oven to 350°.
• In a very small bowl, whisk together remaining 1 tablespoon cream and remaining ¼ teaspoon honey. Brush tops of scones with cream mixture and sprinkle with remaining ½ teaspoon lavender.
• Bake until edges of scones are golden brown, 15 to 18 minutes. Serve warm or at room temperature.

We used King Arthur Gluten Free Measure for Measure Flour.
†*See note about freezing scones on page 94.*

RECOMMENDED CONDIMENTS:
Lemon curd | Raspberry jam

Elderflower-Apricot Gluten-free Scones
Makes 11 to 13

Elderflower, an iconic British flavor, melds wonderfully with dried apricot for a delectable, gluten-free scone that is terrific for any teatime.

2½ cups gluten-free all-purpose baking flour blend*
4 teaspoons baking powder
½ teaspoon fine sea salt
5 tablespoons unsalted butter, cubed
¼ cup plus 2 tablespoons caster sugar
½ cup chopped dried apricots
3 medium eggs, beaten, divided
¾ cup whole milk, divided
½ teaspoon elderflower extract**
¼ teaspoon vanilla extract

• Line a rimmed baking sheet with parchment paper.
• In a large bowl, whisk together flour, baking powder, and salt. Using fingers, rub in butter as lightly as possible until mixture resembles coarse crumbs. Stir in sugar, and then stir in apricots.
• In a medium bowl, whisk together 2 eggs, ½ cup plus 2 tablespoons milk, and extracts. Add to flour mixture, stirring until a dough begins to form. Working gently, bring mixture together in bowl with hands until a dough forms.
• Turn out dough onto a floured* surface, and knead gently by patting dough and folding it in half 5 or 6 times. Using a rolling pin, roll out dough to a 1-inch thickness. Using a 2-inch round cutter dipped in flour*, cut as many scones as possible from dough without twisting cutter, rerolling scraps as necessary. Place scones on prepared baking sheet. Let scones rest at room temperature for at least 30 minutes and up to 1 hour.
• Preheat oven to 400°.
• In a small bowl, whisk together remaining egg and remaining 2 tablespoons milk to make an egg wash. Brush egg wash over tops of scones.
• Bake until scones are lightly golden brown, 16 to 18 minutes. Serve warm or at room temperature.

We used Bob's Red Mill Gluten Free 1-to-1 Baking Flour.
**We used Elderflower Flavor Extract from Olive Nation, olivenation.com or 617-580-3667.*

RECOMMENDED CONDIMENTS:
Clotted cream | Orange marmalade | Apricot jam

½ cup plus 2 tablespoons finely chopped sweetened dried pineapple, divided
⅓ cup chopped macadamia nuts, toasted and cooled
1 cup plus 1 tablespoon cold organic coconut milk, divided
2 tablespoons chopped macadamia nuts

• Line a rimmed baking sheet with parchment paper.
• Place coconut oil in a shallow bowl. Refrigerate until oil begins to solidify, 5 to 10 minutes. Using a fork, score coconut oil deeply to create a fine grid pattern. Refrigerate until firm, 15 to 20 minutes more.
• In a large bowl, whisk together flour, sugar, baking powder, and salt. Using your fingertips, rub in cold coconut oil as lightly as possible until mixture resembles coarse crumbs. Stir in ½ cup pineapple and toasted macadamia nuts.
• Add 1 cup coconut milk to flour mixture, stirring until a dough begins to form. Working gently and quickly, bring mixture together in bowl with hands until a dough forms. (If dough won't come together, add more coconut milk, 1 tablespoon at a time, until it does. Dough should be somewhat firm.)
• Turn out dough onto a lightly floured* surface, and gently knead by patting dough and folding it in half 4 or 5 times. Using a rolling pin, roll out dough to a 1-inch thickness. Using a 2½-inch flower-shaped cutter dipped in flour*, cut as many scones as possible from dough without twisting cutter, rerolling scraps as necessary. Place scones on prepared baking sheet. Freeze scones for at least 15 minutes†.
• Preheat oven to 400°.
• Brush tops of frozen scones with remaining 1 tablespoon coconut milk.
• In a small bowl, stir together macadamia nuts and remaining 2 tablespoons pineapple. Divide mixture evenly among centers of scones, mounding slightly.
• Bake until edges of scones are golden brown and a wooden pick inserted in the centers comes out clean, 15 to 18 minutes. Serve warm or at room temperature.

*We recommend dairy-free and gluten-free flour blends such as King Arthur Gluten Free Measure for Measure Flour or Bob's Red Mill Gluten Free 1-to-1 Baking Flour.
†See note about freezing scones on page 94.

RECOMMENDED CONDIMENT:
Orange marmalade

Pineapple, Macadamia & Coconut Dairy-free Scones
Makes 13 to 15

The iconic flavors of Hawaii in these gluten-free, vegan scones are sure to please your ohana at teatime or anytime. We recommend pairing this tropical treat with a refreshing and fruity tea blend of your choice, perhaps an oolong with notes of citrus.

6 tablespoons virgin unrefined coconut oil
2 cups gluten-free all-purpose flour blend*
¼ cup golden coconut sugar, sifted
2 teaspoons baking powder
½ teaspoon fine sea salt

Ginger-Peach Gluten-free Scones
Makes 11 to 13

Herbal tea adds remarkable flavor to these tasty scones that are studded with peach and crystallized ginger, creating the ideal summertime treat.

6 tea bags ginger-peach herbal tea*
1¼ cups heavy whipping cream
2 (4-ounce) containers chopped peaches in 100% juice, well drained (approximately ⅔ cup)
2½ cups gluten-free all-purpose flour blend for baking**
⅓ cup granulated sugar
1 tablespoon baking powder
½ teaspoon fine sea salt
6 tablespoons cold unsalted butter, cubed
3 tablespoons minced crystalized ginger
1 large egg

• Place tea bags in a small bowl. Add cream, cover bowl, and let steep for at least 3 hours in the refrigerator. Gently squeeze and discard tea bags. Return cream to refrigerator to keep cold.
• Preheat oven to 400°. Line a rimmed baking sheet with parchment paper.
• Blot peaches well with paper towels. Coarsely chop peaches.
• In a large bowl, whisk together flour, sugar, baking powder, and salt. Using a pastry blender or 2 forks, cut butter into flour mixture until it resembles coarse crumbs. Stir in ginger and peaches.
• Add egg to chilled cream, whisking well. Gradually add ¾ cup cream mixture to flour mixture, stirring until a shaggy dough begins to form. Working gently, bring mixture together in bowl with hands until a dough forms. (If dough won't come together, add more cream mixture, 1 tablespoon at a time, until it does. Dough should be somewhat firm.)
• Turn out dough onto a lightly floured surface**, and knead gently until somewhat smooth by patting dough and folding it in half 3 to 4 times. Using a rolling pin, roll dough to a ¾- to 1-inch thickness. Using a 2-inch fluted round cutter dipped in flour**, cut as many scones as possible from dough without twisting cutter, rerolling scraps as necessary. Place scones 1 inch apart on prepared baking sheet. Freeze for 15 minutes†.
• Brush top of scones with remaining cream mixture.

• Bake until edges of scones are golden brown, approximately 20 minutes. Serve warm.

*We used Bigelow Benefits Ginger & Peach Herbal Tea.
**We used Bob's Red Mill Gluten Free 1-to-1 Baking Flour.
†See note about freezing scones on page 94.

RECOMMENDED CONDIMENTS:
Clotted cream | Lemon curd | Orange marmalade

Pumpkin-Date Gluten-free Scones
Makes 14

Loaded with moist pumpkin and an array of spices, these date-studded scones are delicious accompaniments for teatime in the fall.

2 cups gluten-free all-purpose flour blend*
⅓ cup granulated sugar
2 teaspoons baking powder
¾ teaspoon ground cinnamon
½ teaspoon fine sea salt
½ teaspoon ground allspice
½ teaspoon ground ginger
¼ teaspoon ground nutmeg
4 tablespoons cold salted butter, cubed
½ cup chopped dates
¾ cup cold heavy whipping cream
½ cup canned pumpkin puree
½ teaspoon vanilla extract
Garnish: additional granulated sugar

• Preheat oven to 350°. Line a rimmed baking sheet with parchment paper.
• In a large bowl, whisk together flour, sugar, baking powder, cinnamon, salt, allspice, ginger, and nutmeg.

Using a pastry blender or 2 forks, cut butter into flour mixture until it resembles coarse crumbs. Stir in dates.
• In a small bowl, whisk together cream, pumpkin puree, and vanilla extract. Add to flour mixture, stirring until a dough begins to form. Working gently, bring mixture together in bowl with hands until a dough forms. (If dough won't come together, add more cream, 1 table-spoon at a time, until it does. Dough should be some-what firm.)
• Turn out dough onto a lightly floured* surface, and knead gently until smooth by patting dough and folding it in half 4 to 5 times. Using a rolling pin, roll out dough to a ¾-inch thickness. Using a 2¼-inch round cutter dipped in flour*, cut 14 scones from dough without twisting cutter, rerolling scraps as necessary. Place scones 2 inches apart on prepared baking sheet.
• Garnish scones with a sprinkle of sugar, if desired.
• Bake until edges of scones are golden brown and a wooden pick inserted in the centers comes out clean, 18 to 20 minutes.

We used Cup4Cup Gluten Free Multipurpose Flour, available at Williams-Sonoma, Sur la Table, Walgreens, and amazon.com, among others.

RECOMMENDED CONDIMENT:
Faux Clotted Cream (recipe on page 122)

Cranberry-Chai Gluten-free Scones
Makes 8 to 10

Toothsome scones laden with dried cranberries and the marvelous flavors of masala chai present a tempting bake that is equal parts sweet and spicy.

¾ cup whole milk
3 tablespoons masala chai loose-leaf tea
2½ cups gluten-free all-purpose baking flour*
4 teaspoons baking powder
½ teaspoon fine sea salt
5 tablespoons unsalted butter, cubed
¼ cup plus 1 tablespoon granulated sugar, divided
½ cup dried cranberries
2 medium eggs
½ teaspoon vanilla extract

• In a pint jar with a lid, combine milk and loose-leaf tea. Cover and refrigerate for at least 6 hours.
• Line a rimmed baking sheet with parchment paper.
• In a large bowl, whisk together flour, baking powder, and salt. Using fingers, rub in butter as lightly as possible until mixture resembles coarse crumbs. Stir in ¼ cup sugar, and then stir in cranberries.
• Using an infuser basket or a very fine–mesh sieve, strain infused milk into a liquid-measuring cup, discarding tea leaves.
• In a medium bowl, whisk together eggs, ½ cup plus 2 tablespoons infused milk, and vanilla extract. Add to flour mixture, stirring until a dough begins to form. Working gently, bring mixture together in bowl with hands until a dough forms.
• Turn out dough onto a floured* surface, and knead gently by patting dough and folding it in half 3 or 4 times. Using a rolling pin, roll out dough to a 1-inch thickness. Using a 2½-inch fluted round cutter dipped in flour*, cut as many scones as possible from dough without twisting cutter, rerolling scraps as necessary. Place scones, evenly spaced, on prepared baking sheet. Freeze for at least 30 minutes†.
• Preheat oven to 400°.
• Sprinkle tops of scones with remaining 1 tablespoon sugar.
• Bake until scones are lightly golden brown, 16 to 18 minutes. Serve immediately.

*We used Bob's Red Mill Gluten Free 1-to-1 Baking Flour.
†See note about freezing scones on page 94.

RECOMMENDED CONDIMENTS:
Clotted cream | Orange marmalade

Peanut Butter & Chocolate Gluten-free Scones

Makes 16 to 18

Studded with peanut butter morsels, these decadent scones get their chocolaty flavor from cocoa powder incorporated into the dough. Resist the urge to roll the dough any thicker than ½ inch, though, as the scones will likely not hold their shape, and don't skip the freezing step.

2 cups gluten-free all-purpose flour blend*
⅓ cup granulated sugar
3 tablespoons unsweetened cocoa powder
1 tablespoon baking powder
½ teaspoon fine sea salt
6 tablespoons cold unsalted butter, cubed
½ cup peanut butter chips
1½ cups plus 1 tablespoon cold heavy whipping cream, divided
½ teaspoon vanilla extract
Garnish: additional granulated sugar

• Preheat oven to 350°. Line 2 rimmed baking sheets with parchment paper.
• In a large bowl, whisk together flour, sugar, cocoa powder, baking powder, and salt. Using a pastry blender or 2 forks, cut butter into flour mixture until it resembles coarse crumbs. Stir in peanut butter chips.
• In a liquid-measuring cup, stir together 1½ cups cream and vanilla extract. Add to flour mixture, stirring until a dough begins to form. Working gently, bring mixture together in bowl with hands until a dough forms.
• Turn out dough onto a lightly floured* surface, and knead gently until smooth by patting dough and folding it in half 4 to 5 times. Using a rolling pin, roll out dough to a ½-inch thickness. Using a 2¼-inch round cutter dipped in flour*, cut as many scones as possible from dough without twisting cutter, rerolling scraps as necessary. Place scones 2 inches apart on prepared baking sheets. Freeze scones for at least 15 minutes†.
• Brush tops of cold scones with remaining 1 tablespoon cream. Garnish tops of scones with a sprinkle of sugar, if desired.
• Bake until edges of scones are golden brown, approximately 20 minutes. Let cool for at least 5 minutes before serving.

*We used King Arthur Gluten Free Measure for Measure Flour.
†See note about freezing scones on page 94.

RECOMMENDED CONDIMENTS:
Clotted cream | Strawberry jam

Chocolate-Hazelnut Gluten-free Scones
Makes 14

An indulgent treat for teatime and beyond, these pretty scones pack supreme decadence in petite packages.

2 cups gluten-free all-purpose flour blend
½ cup plus 1 tablespoon granulated sugar, divided
2¼ teaspoons baking powder
½ teaspoon xanthan gum*
½ teaspoon fine sea salt
4 tablespoons cold unsalted butter, cubed
⅓ cup chopped toasted hazelnuts
½ cup dark chocolate chips
1 cup plus 1 tablespoon cold heavy whipping cream,
    divided
½ teaspoon vanilla extract

• Preheat oven to 350°. Line a rimmed baking sheet with parchment paper.
• In a medium bowl, whisk together flour, ½ cup sugar, baking powder, xanthan gum, and salt. Using a pastry blender or 2 forks, cut butter into flour mixture until it resembles coarse crumbs. Stir in hazelnuts and chocolate.
• In a small bowl, stir together 1 cup cream and vanilla extract. Add to flour mixture, stirring until a shaggy dough begins to form. Working gently, bring mixture together in bowl with hands until a dough forms. (If dough won't come together, add more cream, 1 tablespoon at a time, until it does. Dough should be somewhat firm.)
• Turn out dough onto a lightly floured** surface, and knead gently until smooth by patting dough and folding it in half 2 to 3 times. Using a rolling pin, roll out dough to a 1-inch thickness. Using a 2-inch fluted square cutter dipped in flour**, cut 14 scones from dough without twisting cutter, rerolling scraps as necessary. Place scones 2 inches apart on prepared baking sheets.
• Brush tops of scones with remaining 1 tablespoon cream.
• Bake until edges of scones are light golden brown and a wooden pick inserted in the centers comes out clean, 20 to 23 minutes. Serve warm or at room temperature.

*May omit if flour blend already includes this.
**We used gluten-free all-purpose flour blend.

RECOMMENDED CONDIMENTS:
Faux Clotted Cream (recipe on page 122) | Raspberry jam

Blueberry, Chamomile & White Chocolate Gluten-free Scones

Makes approximately 12

Chamomile isn't just for sipping at bedtime. It is a key ingredient and garnish in this whimsically shaped scone laced with freeze-dried blueberries and creamy white chocolate.

2¾ cups gluten-free all-purpose baking flour blend*
¼ cup caster sugar
4 teaspoons baking powder
½ teaspoon fine sea salt
5 tablespoons unsalted butter, cubed
½ cup freeze-dried organic blueberries
2 ounces white chocolate baking bar, finely chopped
¼ cup (4 grams) dried chamomile
2 large eggs, lightly beaten
¾ cup cold whole milk, divided
¼ teaspoon vanilla extract

• Line a rimmed baking sheet with parchment paper.
• In a large bowl, whisk together flour, sugar, baking powder, and salt. Using fingers, rub in butter as lightly as possible until mixture resembles coarse crumbs. Stir in blueberries and white chocolate.
• Place chamomile in a fine-mesh sieve. Using the back of a spoon, press chamomile through sieve and into a small bowl, discarding large stems. Add 1 tablespoon chamomile to flour mixture, stirring until combined.
• In a medium bowl, whisk together eggs, ½ cup plus 2 tablespoons milk, and vanilla extract. Add to flour mixture, stirring until a dough begins to form. Working gently, bring mixture together in bowl with hands until a dough forms.
• Turn out dough onto a lightly floured* surface, and knead gently until smooth by patting dough and folding it in half 6 to 8 times. Using a rolling pin, roll out dough to a ¾-inch thickness. Using a 2¾-inch flower-shaped cutter dipped in flour*, cut as many scones as possible from dough without twisting cutter, rerolling scraps as necessary. Place scones, evenly spaced, on prepared baking sheet. Freeze scones for 20 minutes†.
• Preheat oven to 350°.
• Brush tops of cold scones with remaining 2 tablespoons milk. Sprinkle remaining chamomile in a circle in center of scones.

• Bake until edges of scones are lightly golden brown, 15 to 20 minutes. Serve immediately.

*We used King Arthur Gluten Free Measure for Measure Flour.
†See note about freezing scones on page 94.

RECOMMENDED CONDIMENT:
Lemon Curd (recipe on page 128)

Cherry-Almond Low-Carb Scones
Makes 8

A treat for those following a low-carbohydrate or gluten-free diet, hearty scones made with almond and coconut flours are packed with luscious cream cheese and sweet dried cherries.

2¾ cups plus 2 tablespoons almond flour, divided
¼ cup coconut flour
½ teaspoon baking soda
½ teaspoon fine sea salt
2 tablespoons cold unsalted butter, cubed
2 ounces cold cream cheese, cubed
½ cup dried cherries
⅓ cup sliced almonds, crushed
2 large eggs
3 tablespoons heavy whipping cream, divided
1 tablespoon honey
1¼ teaspoons almond extract
Garnish: coconut sugar

• Preheat oven to 375°. Line a rimmed baking sheet with parchment paper.
• In a large bowl, whisk together 2¾ cups almond flour, coconut flour, baking soda, and salt. Using a pastry blender or 2 forks, cut in butter until it resembles coarse crumbs. Add cream cheese, stirring until coated with flours. Stir in cherries.
• In a small bowl, whisk together eggs, 2 tablespoons heavy cream, honey, and almond extract. Add egg mixture to flour mixture, stirring until a dough forms. Refrigerate dough for 15 minutes. (This is important, as it allows coconut flour to absorb moisture.)
• Sprinkle remaining 2 tablespoons almond flour on a

work surface. Shape dough into a ball and place on pre-pared work surface. Using a rolling pin, roll out dough to a 1-inch-thick circle. Using a large chef 's knife, cut dough circle into 8 wedges. Place scones 2 inches apart on prepared baking sheet.
• Brush tops of scones with remaining 1 tablespoon heavy cream. Garnish scones with a sprinkling of coco-nut sugar, if desired.
• Bake until edges and bottoms of scones are light golden brown, 10 to 15 minutes. Serve warm or at room temperature.

EDITOR'S NOTE: This dough also works well for round cutout scones. A 2¼-inch round cutter yields 8 to 10 scones. Bake as indicated in recipe.

RECOMMENDED CONDIMENT:
Unsweetened whipped cream or Clotted cream

- Preheat oven to 350°. Line a rimmed baking sheet with parchment paper.
- In a large bowl, whisk together flour, sugar, baking powder, and salt. Using a pastry blender or 2 forks, cut butter into flour mixture until it resembles coarse crumbs. Stir in cranberries and almonds.
- In a small bowl, stir together 1¼ cups plus 2 table-spoons cream, vanilla extract, and almond extract. Add to flour mixture, stirring until dough comes together.
- Using a levered 3-tablespoon scoop, drop dough 2 inches apart onto prepared baking sheet.
- Bake until edges of scones are golden brown and a wooden pick inserted in the centers comes out clean, approximately 20 minutes.

RECOMMENDED CONDIMENTS:

Clotted cream | Lemon curd

Cranberry-Almond Gluten-free Drop Scones

Makes 17

These toothsome drop scones, flavored by dried cranberries and toasted almonds, are a nice and uncomplicated option for a casual teatime.

2 cups gluten-free all-purpose flour blend
⅓ cup granulated sugar
2 teaspoons baking powder
½ teaspoon fine sea salt
4 tablespoons cold unsalted butter, cubed
½ cup dried cranberries
⅓ cup chopped toasted almonds
1¼ cups plus 3 tablespoons cold heavy whipping cream, divided
½ teaspoon vanilla extract
¼ teaspoon almond extract

Almond Sugar-free Scones

Makes 12

A diabetic-friendly alternative replaces conventional granulated sugar in these delightful scones that pay homage to classic almond sugar cookies but with an added zing from ginger paste.

2½ cups all-purpose flour
⅓ cup granulated sugar substitute*
2½ teaspoons baking powder
¾ teaspoon fine sea salt
½ cup cold unsalted butter, cubed
¼ cup toasted sliced almonds
½ cup cold whole milk
2 large eggs, lightly beaten, divided
1¼ teaspoons ginger paste
1 teaspoon vanilla extract
¾ teaspoon almond extract
12 whole blanched almonds

- Preheat oven to 375°. Line a rimmed baking sheet with parchment paper.
- In a large bowl, whisk together flour, sugar substitute, baking powder, and salt. Using a pastry blender or 2 forks,

cut butter into flour mixture until it resembles coarse crumbs. Gently stir in sliced almonds until incorporated.

• In a medium bowl, whisk together milk, 1 egg, ginger paste, vanilla extract, and almond extract. Add milk mixture to flour mixture, stirring until a shaggy dough begins to form. Working gently, bring mixture together in bowl with hands until a dough forms. (If dough won't come together, add more milk, 1 tablespoon at a time, until it does. Dough should be somewhat firm.)

• Turn out dough onto a lightly floured surface, and knead gently until smooth by patting dough and folding it in half 3 to 5 times. Using a rolling pin, roll out dough to a ¾-inch thickness. Using a 2-inch round cutter dipped in flour, cut 12 scones from dough without twisting cutter, rerolling scraps as necessary. Place scones 2 inches apart on prepared baking sheet.

• Gently press a whole blanched almond into the top of each scone. Freeze for 15 minutes†.

• Brush tops of scones with remaining 1 egg.

• Bake until scones are lightly browned, 14 to 16 minutes. Remove from oven and let cool on baking sheet for 10 minutes before serving.

*We used Swerve Granular Sugar Replacement.
†See note about freezing scones on page 94.

RECOMMENDED CONDIMENTS:
Clotted cream | Sugar-free raspberry jam

Pear Gluten-free Scones
Makes approximately 18

Bits of fresh Bartlett pear impart the fruit's classic sweetness to the dough of these gluten-free scones, while a touch of cardamom infuses just the right amount of spice.

2¼ cups gluten-free all-purpose flour blend*
¼ cup caster sugar
1 tablespoon baking powder
1 teaspoon fine sea salt
¼ teaspoon ground cardamom
4 tablespoons cold unsalted butter, cubed
1 finely diced peeled slightly firm Bartlett pear
    (approximately 1 cup)
¾ cup plus 1 tablespoon cold heavy whipping cream,
    divided
1 large egg
½ teaspoon vanilla extract

• Preheat oven to 350°. Line a rimmed baking sheet with parchment paper.
• In a large bowl, whisk together flour, sugar, baking powder, salt, and cardamom. Using fingers, rub butter into flour mixture until it resembles coarse crumbs. Stir in pear.
• In a small bowl, whisk together ¾ cup cream, egg, and vanilla extract. Add to flour mixture, stirring until a dough begins to form. Working gently, bring mixture together in bowl with hands until a dough forms. (If dough won't come together, add more cream, 1 tablespoon at a time, until it does. Dough should be somewhat firm.)
• Turn out dough onto a lightly floured* surface, and knead gently by patting dough and folding it in half 3 times. Using a rolling pin, roll out dough to a ¾-inch thickness. Using a 2-inch fluted round cutter dipped in flour*, cut as many scones as possible from dough without twisting cutter, rerolling scraps as necessary. Place scones, evenly spaced, on prepared baking sheet.
• Brush tops of scones with remaining 1 tablespoon cream.
• Bake until edges of scones are golden brown, 20 to 25 minutes. Serve warm or at room temperature.

We used King Arthur Gluten Free Measure for Measure Flour.

RECOMMENDED CONDIMENTS:
Clotted cream | Pear jam

Toasted Pecan Gluten-free Scones
Makes 12

*Pieces of pecan complement the sweet flavor of these
square scones, especially when served with a scrumptious
chai-flavored cream.*

2 cups gluten-free all-purpose flour blend*
⅓ cup firmly packed light brown sugar
2 teaspoons baking powder
½ teaspoon fine sea salt
6 tablespoons cold unsalted butter, cubed
½ cup coarsely chopped toasted pecans
¾ cup cold heavy whipping cream
½ teaspoon vanilla extract
Garnish: turbinado sugar and chopped pecans

• Preheat oven to 350°. Line a rimmed baking sheet
with parchment paper.
• In a large bowl, whisk together flour, sugar, baking
powder, and salt. Using a pastry blender or 2 forks,
cut butter into flour mixture until it resembles coarse
crumbs. Stir in toasted pecans.
• In a small bowl, stir together cream and vanilla extract.
Add to flour mixture, stirring until a shaggy dough begins
to form. Working gently, bring mixture together in bowl
with hands until a dough forms. (If dough won't come
together, add more cream, 1 tablespoon at a time, until
it does. Dough should be somewhat firm.)
• Turn out dough onto a lightly floured* surface, and
knead gently until smooth by patting dough and folding
it in half 4 to 5 times. Using a rolling pin, roll out dough
to a 1-inch thickness. Using a 2-inch square cutter
dipped in flour*, cut 12 scones from dough without
twisting cutter, rerolling scraps as necessary. Place
scones 2 inches apart on prepared baking sheet.
• Garnish tops of scones with turbinado sugar and
pecans, if desired.
• Bake until edges of scones are golden brown and a
wooden pick inserted in the centers comes out clean,
approximately 20 minutes.

We used Bob's Red Mill Gluten Free 1-to-1 Baking Flour.

RECOMMENDED CONDIMENT:
Chai-infused Cream (recipe on page 123)

Toffee-Pecan Gluten-free Scones
Makes 13

With delectable sweetness from toffee bits and desirable crunch from toasted pecans, this irresistible taste combination will quickly become a favorite.

2 cups gluten-free all-purpose flour blend
¼ cup granulated sugar
2 teaspoons baking powder
½ teaspoon fine sea salt
4 tablespoons cold unsalted butter, cubed
⅓ cup toffee bits
⅓ cup chopped toasted pecans
1 cup plus 1 tablespoon cold heavy whipping cream, divided
½ teaspoon vanilla extract
Garnish: turbinado sugar

• Preheat oven to 350°. Line a rimmed baking sheet with parchment paper.
• In a large bowl, whisk together flour, granulated sugar, baking powder, and salt. Using a pastry blender or 2 forks, cut butter into flour mixture until it resembles coarse crumbs. Stir in toffee bits and pecans.
• In a liquid-measuring cup, stir together 1 cup cream and vanilla extract. Add to flour mixture, stirring until a shaggy dough begins to form. Working gently, bring mixture together in bowl with hands until a dough forms. (If dough won't come together, add more cream, 1 tablespoon at a time, until it does. Dough should be somewhat firm.)
• Turn out dough onto a lightly floured* surface, and knead gently until smooth by patting dough and folding it in half 4 to 5 times. Using a rolling pin, roll out dough to a ¾-inch thickness. Using a 2-inch square cutter dipped in flour*, cut 13 scones from dough without twisting cutter, rerolling scraps as necessary. Place scones 2 inches apart on prepared baking sheet.
• Brush tops of scones with remaining 1 tablespoon cream. Garnish tops of scones with a sprinkle of turbinado sugar, if desired.
• Bake until edges of scones are golden brown and a wooden pick inserted in the centers comes out clean, 18 to 20 minutes.

*We used gluten-free all-purpose flour blend.

RECOMMENDED CONDIMENT:
Faux Clotted Cream (recipe on page 122)

Gingerbread Gluten-free Scones
Makes 16

Savor old-fashioned Christmas flavors in these festive and delicious scones filled with notes of ginger, nutmeg, molasses, and vanilla. Add a bit of zing to the sweet pastry with a dollop of lemon curd.

2 cups gluten-free all-purpose flour blend*
¼ cup firmly packed light brown sugar
2 tablespoons finely chopped crystalized ginger
2 tablespoons natural unsweetened cocoa powder
2 teaspoons baking powder
1½ teaspoons ground ginger
1 teaspoon ground Vietnamese cinnamon
½ teaspoon fine sea salt
⅛ teaspoon ground cloves
⅛ teaspoon ground nutmeg
⅛ teaspoon ground black pepper
4 tablespoons cold salted butter, cubed
½ cup cold heavy whipping cream
⅓ cup molasses
½ teaspoon vanilla extract
Garnish: confectioners' sugar

• Preheat oven to 350°. Line a rimmed baking sheet with parchment paper.
• In a large bowl, whisk together flour, brown sugar, crystalized ginger, cocoa powder, baking powder, ground ginger, cinnamon, salt, cloves, nutmeg, and pepper, whisking well. Using a pastry blender or 2 forks, cut butter into flour mixture until it resembles coarse crumbs.
• In a small bowl, whisk together cream, molasses, and vanilla extract. Add to flour mixture, stirring until a shaggy dough begins to form. Working gently, bring mixture together in bowl with hands until a dough forms. (If dough won't come together, add more cream, 1 tablespoon at a time, until it does. Dough should be somewhat firm.)
• Turn out dough onto a lightly floured* surface, and knead gently until smooth by patting dough and folding it in half 3 to 4 times. Using a rolling pin, roll out dough to a ½-inch thickness. Using a 2¼-inch fluted round cutter dipped in flour*, cut 16 scones from dough without twisting cutter, rerolling scraps as necessary. Place scones 2 inches apart on prepared baking sheet.
• Bake until edges of scones are golden brown and a wooden pick inserted in the centers comes out clean, 18 to 20 minutes. Let cool slightly.

• Garnish tops of scones with a dusting of confectioners' sugar, if desired.

We used Glutino Gluten Free Pantry All Purpose Flour.

RECOMMENDED CONDIMENT:
Lemon curd

Apple Pie Gluten-free Scones
Makes 8

Layers of tangy buttermilk scone dough envelop a cooked apple filling laced with warm spices for a gluten-free treat to remember. Serve with our homemade Vanilla Cream for a luxurious indulgence.

8 tablespoons cold unsalted butter, cubed, divided
1 large Granny Smith apple, peeled, cored, and chopped
3 tablespoons dark brown sugar
¾ teaspoon ground cinnamon
¼ teaspoon ground nutmeg
2¼ cups gluten-free all-purpose baking flour blend*
2 tablespoons plus 1 teaspoon granulated sugar, divided
4 teaspoons baking powder
½ teaspoon fine sea salt
¼ teaspoon baking soda
¾ cup plus 1 tablespoon cold whole buttermilk, divided
1 large egg
½ teaspoon vanilla extract

• In a medium skillet over medium-low heat, melt 2 tablespoons butter. Add apple, cooking 1 to 2 minutes, stirring occasionally. Stir in brown sugar, cinnamon, and nutmeg. Cook until apple pieces are slightly tender when pierced with a fork. Transfer apple filling to a heatproof bowl or plate. Refrigerate until cool, at least 30 minutes and up to a day.

• Preheat oven to 375°. Line a rimmed baking sheet with parchment paper.

• In a large bowl, whisk together flour, 2 tablespoons granulated sugar, baking powder, salt, and baking soda. Using a pastry blender or 2 forks, cut remaining 6 table-spoons butter into flour mixture until it resembles coarse crumbs.

• In a medium bowl, whisk together ¾ cup buttermilk, egg, and vanilla extract. Add to flour mixture, stirring until a dough begins to form. Working gently, bring mix-ture together in bowl with hands until a dough forms. (If mixture seems dry and dough won't come together, add more buttermilk, 1 tablespoon at a time, until it does.)

• Turn out dough onto a lightly floured* surface, and knead gently until smooth by patting dough and folding it in half 4 to 5 times. Divide dough into 3 equal portions. Using a rolling pin, roll out each dough portion to a 7-inch circle. Spread half of apple filling over a dough circle, leaving a ½-inch border around edge. Top with another dough circle, and spread with remaining apple filling, leaving a ½-inch border around edge. Top with remaining dough circle. Press border lightly to seal in filling. If necessary, lightly roll out dough circle stack to a ¾- to 1-inch thickness. Using a large sharp knife, cut dough circle into 8 wedges. Using a large metal spatula, carefully transfer scones to prepared baking sheet, keeping wedges touching and circle intact.

• Brush tops of scones with remaining 1 tablespoon buttermilk and sprinkle with remaining 1 teaspoon granulated sugar.

• Bake until scones are lightly browned, approximately 20 minutes. Serve warm or at room temperature.

We used King Arthur Gluten Free Measure for Measure Flour.

RECOMMENDED CONDIMENT:
Vanilla Cream (page 122)

Apple-Spice Gluten-free Scones
Makes 12

Laced with warm spices and laden with chopped green apple, this enticing and well-rounded scone is perfect for an autumnal afternoon tea.

2½ cups gluten-free all-purpose flour blend
½ cup plus ½ tablespoon granulated sugar, divided
2½ teaspoons baking powder
1½ teaspoons apple pie spice, divided
½ teaspoon fine sea salt
8 tablespoons cold unsalted butter, cubed
1 cup chopped, peeled Granny Smith apple
¾ cup plus 3 tablespoons cold heavy whipping cream, divided
½ teaspoon vanilla extract

• Preheat oven to 375°. Line a baking sheet with parchment paper.

• In a medium bowl, whisk together flour, ½ cup sugar, baking powder, 1 teaspoon apple pie spice, and salt.

Using a pastry blender or 2 forks, cut butter into flour mixture until it resembles coarse crumbs. Stir in apple.

• In a small bowl, stir together ¾ cup plus 2 tablespoons cream and vanilla extract. Add to flour mixture, stirring until a shaggy dough begins to form. Working gently, bring mixture together in bowl with hands until a dough forms. (If dough won't come together, add more cream, 1 tablespoon at a time, until it does. Dough should be somewhat firm.)

• Turn out dough onto a lightly floured* surface, and knead gently until smooth by patting dough and folding it in half 3 to 4 times. Using a rolling pin, roll out dough to a 1-inch thickness. Using a 2½-inch round cutter dipped in flour*, cut 12 scones from dough without twisting cutter, rerolling scraps as necessary. Place scones 2 inches apart on prepared baking sheet.

• Brush tops of scones with remaining 1 table-spoon cream.

• In a small bowl, stir together remaining ½ tablespoon sugar and remaining ½ teaspoon apple pie spice. Sprinkle sugar mixture over tops of scones.

• Bake until edges of scones are golden brown and a wooden pick inserted in the centers comes out clean, 20 to 23 minutes. Serve warm.

We used gluten-free all-purpose flour blend.

RECOMMENDED CONDIMENT:
Sweetened Whipped Cream (recipe on page 122)

Apple, Pecan & Cheddar Gluten-free Scones
Makes 14

The classic combination of fruit, nuts, and cheese in these autumn-inspired scones creates a delectable pastry for a tea party.

5 tablespoons cold unsalted butter, divided
1¼ cups diced peeled Granny Smith apple
1 tablespoon granulated sugar
2¼ cups gluten-free all-purpose baking flour blend*
¼ cup firmly packed light brown sugar
1 tablespoon baking powder
½ teaspoon fine sea salt
½ cup coarsely shredded sharp Cheddar cheese
⅓ cup chopped toasted pecans
1¼ cups plus 1 tablespoon cold heavy whipping cream, divided
¼ teaspoon vanilla extract

• In a medium sauté pan, melt 1 tablespoon butter over medium heat. Add apple and granulated sugar, stirring well. Cook, covered, stirring frequently, until apple pieces are tender and lightly browned, approximately 5 minutes. Transfer cooked apple to a heatproof bowl. Let come to room temperature.
• Preheat oven to 400°. Line a rimmed baking sheet with parchment paper.
• In a large bowl, whisk together flour, brown sugar, baking powder, and salt. Using a pastry blender or 2 forks, cut in remaining 4 tablespoons butter until it resembles coarse crumbs. Stir in cooled apple, cheese, and pecans.
• In a small bowl, stir together 1¼ cups cream and vanilla extract. Add cream mixture to flour mixture, stirring until a shaggy dough begins to form. Working gently, bring mixture together in bowl with hands until a dough forms. (If dough won't come together, add more cream, 1 tablespoon at a time, until it does. Dough should be somewhat firm.)
• Turn out dough onto a lightly floured* surface, and knead gently until smooth by patting dough and folding it in half 4 to 5 times. Using a rolling pin, roll out dough to a 1-inch thickness. Using a 2¼-inch round cutter dipped in flour*, cut 14 scones from dough without twisting cutter, rerolling scraps as necessary. Place scones 2 inches apart on prepared baking sheet.

- Brush tops of scones with remaining 1 tablespoon cream.
- Bake until edges of scones are golden brown and a wooden pick inserted in the centers comes out clean, approximately 13 minutes. Serve warm.

Gluten-free flour blends such as Bob's Red Mill Gluten Free 1-to-1 Baking Flour, Cup4Cup Gluten Free Multipurpose Flour, or King Arthur's Gluten Free Measure for Measure Flour are best for these scones.

RECOMMENDED CONDIMENT:
Clotted cream

Fig & Blue Cheese Gluten-free Drop Scones
Makes 24 to 26

Imparted with the sweet flavor of dried figs and the savory taste of blue cheese crumbles, these dynamic and brilliantly nuanced drop scones will undoubtedly become a huge hit at your next afternoon tea.

3 cups gluten-free all-purpose flour blend*
4½ teaspoons baking powder
½ teaspoon fine sea salt
8 tablespoons cold salted butter, cubed
1 cup chopped dried figs
½ cup gluten-free blue cheese crumbles**
1¾ cups cold heavy whipping cream
1 large egg
2 tablespoons turbinado sugar

- Preheat oven to 400°. Line 2 rimmed baking sheets with parchment paper.
- In a large bowl, whisk together flour, baking powder, and salt. Using a pastry blender or 2 forks, cut butter into flour mixture until it resembles coarse crumbs. Stir in figs and blue cheese.
- In a small bowl, whisk together cream and egg. Add to flour mixture, stirring until a dough forms.
- Using a levered 3-tablespoon scoop, drop dough, evenly spaced, onto prepared baking sheets. Sprinkle tops of scones with turbinado sugar.
- Bake until scones are light golden brown and a

wooden pick inserted in the centers comes out clean, 13 to 15 minutes. Serve warm.

We used Glutino Gluten Free Pantry All Purpose Flour.
***We suggest using Organic Valley or Alouette blue cheese crumbles.*

RECOMMENDED CONDIMENTS:
Faux Clotted Cream (recipe on page 122) | Orange marmalade

Irish Cheddar, Ham & Chive Gluten-free Low-Carb Scones
Makes 8

Served warm with mustard or clotted cream, these luscious wedge scones are perfect for anyone following a keto diet.

2¾ cup almond flour
¼ cup coconut flour
1 tablespoon baking powder
½ teaspoon fine sea salt
4 tablespoons unsalted Irish butter*
½ cup shredded Irish Cheddar cheese*
½ cup cooked diced ham
¼ cup diced fresh chives
¼ cup plus 2 tablespoons cold heavy whipping cream, divided
2 eggs
Garnish: everything bagel seasoning

• Preheat oven to 350°. Line a rimmed baking sheet with parchment paper.
• In a large bowl, whisk together almond flour, coconut flour, baking powder, and salt. Using a pastry blender or 2 forks, cut butter into flour mixture until it resembles coarse crumbs. Stir in cheese, ham, and chives.
• In a small bowl, whisk together ¼ cup cream and eggs until lightly blended. Add to flour mixture, stirring until a dough forms.
• Turn out dough onto a lightly floured** surface and shape into a 1½-inch-thick circle. Using a sharp knife, cut dough circle into 8 wedges. Place scones, evenly spaced, on prepared baking sheet.
• Brush tops of scones with remaining 2 tablespoons cream. Garnish scones with a sprinkle of everything bagel seasoning, if desired.
• Bake until scones are lightly browned, 20 to 25 minutes. Serve warm.

*We used Kerrygold.
**We used almond flour.

RECOMMENDED CONDIMENTS:
Yellow mustard | Clotted cream

Bacon-Butternut Gluten-free Scones
Makes 8 to 10

Bits of bacon and a comforting butternut squash purée add depth of flavor to this savory seasonal scone. The charming leaf shape is sure to delight teatime guests and is the perfect addition to an autumnal menu.

2¾ cups gluten-free all-purpose flour blend*
2 tablespoons firmly packed dark brown sugar
2 teaspoons baking powder
¾ teaspoon fine sea salt
¼ teaspoon baking soda
6 tablespoons cold unsalted butter, cubed
3 slices bacon, cooked, cooled, and crumbled
¾ cup butternut squash purée**
1 large egg, lightly beaten
½ cup plus 2 tablespoons cold whole buttermilk, divided

• Preheat oven to 400°. Line a rimmed baking sheet with parchment paper.
• In a large bowl, whisk together flour, brown sugar, baking powder, salt, and baking soda. Using a pastry blender or 2 forks, cut butter into flour mixture until it resembles coarse crumbs. Stir in bacon.
• In a small bowl, stir together squash purée and egg. Add to flour mixture, stirring with a fork. Stir in ½ cup buttermilk. Working gently, bring mixture together in bowl with hands until a dough forms. (If dough won't come together, add more buttermilk, 1 tablespoon at a time, until it does. Dough should be somewhat firm.)
• Turn out dough onto a lightly floured* surface, and knead gently by patting dough and folding it in half 4 or 5 times. Using a rolling pin, roll out dough to a ¾-inch thickness. Using a 3-inch leaf-shaped cutter dipped in flour*, cut as many scones as possible from dough without twisting cutter, rerolling scraps as necessary. Place scones, almost touching, on prepared baking sheet. Brush tops of scones with remaining 2 table-spoons buttermilk.
• Bake until scones are firm and light golden, 13 to 15 minutes. Serve warm.

*We used Cup4Cup Gluten Free Multipurpose Flour.
**For purée, cut a small butternut squash in half and remove seeds. Rub cut sides of squash with olive oil. Place squash, cut side down, on a foil-lined rimmed baking sheet. Bake at 400° until tender, 20 to 25 minutes. Let cool completely. Scoop flesh from shells, discarding shells. In the work bowl of a food processor or the container of a blender, purée squash flesh. Transfer purée to a coffee filter–lined strainer. Set strainer over a bowl and refrigerate for 4 hours. Discard any strained juices.

RECOMMENDED CONDIMENT:
Rosemary-Honey Butter (recipe on page 126)

Spreads

LUSCIOUS CREAMS, FLAVORFUL BUTTERS,
ZESTY CURDS, AND FRUITY JAMS ADD
SCRUMPTIOUS SWEETNESS OR SAVORY ZING
TO TOOTHSOME SCONES.

Faux Clotted Cream
Makes 1 cup

The traditional teatime condiment that everyone knows and loves is easy to prepare in this simple recipe that mimics the taste and consistency of the real thing.

½ cup cold heavy whipping cream
1 tablespoon confectioners' sugar
1 tablespoon sour cream

• In a small mixing bowl, beat together cream and confectioners' sugar with a mixer at high speed until soft peaks form. Beat in sour cream at low speed until incorporated. Serve immediately, or cover, refrigerate, and use within a day.

Sweetened Whipped Cream
Makes 1½ cups

This simple whipped cream topping is best when made shortly before serving.

1 cup cold heavy whipping cream
3 tablespoons confectioners' sugar
½ teaspoon vanilla extract

• In a small bowl, beat together cream, confectioners' sugar, and vanilla extract with a mixer at high speed until thickened. Use immediately.

Vanilla Cream
Makes 1½ cups

This sumptuous spread is phenomenal on our Apple Pie Gluten-free Scones (page 115) as well as on cakes, cupcakes, and other sweet fare.

2 ounces cream cheese, softened
¾ cup cold heavy whipping cream
2 teaspoons confectioners' sugar
½ teaspoon vanilla extract

• In a large bowl, beat cream cheese with a mixer at medium speed until smooth. Gradually beat in whipping cream, increasing speed to high as needed until soft

CREAM CHEESE SPREAD

peaks form. Beat in confectioners' sugar and vanilla extract until well blended. Cover, refrigerate until needed, and use within 2 days.

Cream Cheese Spread
Makes approximately 1¼ cups

A rich and decadent twist on traditional cream cheese frosting, this spread is perfect for pairing with lightly sweetened scones that mimic the flavors of carrot cake (page 64).

4 ounces cream cheese
2 cups confectioners' sugar
1 tablespoon cold heavy whipping cream
1 teaspoon vanilla extract

• In a medium bowl, beat cream cheese with a mixer at medium speed until smooth. Add confectioners' sugar, 1 cup at a time, beating at low speed until well combined. Add heavy cream and vanilla extract, beating at medium speed until smooth. Cover, refrigerate until needed, and use within 2 days.

Spiced Cream
Makes 2 cups

Two types of cinnamon, fresh ginger root, and cloves combine to create this fantastic spicy spread that adds the perfect flavor boost to our Angel Scones (page 21).

1½ cups heavy whipping cream
3 cinnamon sticks
¼ teaspoon whole cloves
¼ teaspoon thinly sliced fresh ginger root
¼ cup confectioners' sugar
½ teaspoon ground cinnamon

• In a small saucepan, combine cream, cinnamon sticks, cloves, and ginger root. Heat over medium-high heat until very hot but not boiling. Remove from heat, cover, and let steep for 30 minutes.
• Strain cream mixture through a fine-mesh sieve into another container. Cover and refrigerate for at least 6 hours.
• In a mixing bowl, beat together cold cream mixture, confectioners' sugar, and ground cinnamon with a mixer at high speed until stiff peaks form. Cover, refrigerate until needed, and use within 2 days.

Chai-infused Cream
Makes 1 cup

Four ingredients are all it takes to produce this condiment that is infused with spiced black tea and is a great accompaniment for our Toasted Pecan Gluten-free Scones (page 112).

1 cup heavy whipping cream
4 tea bags Masala chai tea or 4 heaping teaspoons
    Masala chai tea leaves
1 tablespoon confectioners' sugar
¼ teaspoon vanilla extract

• In a small saucepan, bring cream to a simmer over medium-high heat. Remove from heat. Add tea bags or tea leaves. Cover, and let steep, approximately 15 minutes. Remove tea bags, or strain cream to remove tea leaves.
• Transfer infused cream to a covered container, and refrigerate until very cold, approximately 6 hours.
• In a medium mixing bowl, beat together cold infused cream, confectioners' sugar, and vanilla extract with a mixer at high speed until stiff peaks form. Use immediately, or cover, refrigerate, and use within a few hours.

Vanilla–Crème Fraîche Cream

Makes 2 cups

This sumptuous, tangy condiment is made with only four ingredients and adds desirable sweetness to our European Butter Scones (page 17).

1 cup cold heavy whipping cream
3 tablespoons confectioners' sugar
½ teaspoon vanilla extract
¼ cup cold crème fraîche

• In a medium deep bowl, beat together whipping cream, confectioners' sugar, and vanilla extract with a mixer at high speed until thickened. Beat in crème fraîche until incorporated. Use immediately.

Honeyed Crème Fraîche

Makes 1 cup

Equal amounts of honey and confectioners' sugar sweeten this tangy mixture of crème fraîche and whipping cream. While this topping is sensational with our Almond–Cream Cheese Scones (page 22), it would be equally great on a plethora of other breads and cakes.

⅓ cup cold heavy whipping cream
½ cup cold crème fraîche
1 tablespoon confectioners' sugar
1 tablespoon honey

• In a small deep bowl, beat cream with a mixer at medium-high speed until soft peaks form. Whisk in crème fraîche, confectioners' sugar, and honey until smooth and creamy. Use immediately, or cover, refrigerate, and use within a day.

Mascarpone Cream

Makes 1 cup

Soft, milky, and gently sweet, this exquisite spread has a similar taste to clotted cream but is deliciously different in its own way. We recommend pairing this condiment with decadent Red Velvet Scones (page 52).

1 (8-ounce) carton mascarpone cheese
2 tablespoons cold heavy whipping cream
2 tablespoons confectioners' sugar
½ teaspoon vanilla extract

• In a medium mixing bowl, beat together mascarpone cheese, cream, sugar, and vanilla extract with a mixer at medium speed until smooth and creamy. Cover, refrigerate until needed, and use within 2 days.

Honey-Mascarpone Cream

Makes 1½ cups

Honey gives this sumptuous spread, made from equal parts heavy cream and mascarpone cheese, the right amount of sweetness.

½ cup cold heavy whipping cream
½ cup mascarpone cheese
3 tablespoons honey
½ teaspoon vanilla extract

• In a large bowl, beat cream with a mixer at high speed until thickened. Beat in mascarpone cheese, honey, and vanilla extract at high speed until incorporated and mixture thickens. Cover, refrigerate, and use within 4 days.

HONEY-MASCARPONE CREAM

Creamy Brown Sugar Spread
Makes ½ cup

This luscious topping only requires mixing together four ingredients for a tasty condiment you will want to make time and time again.

4 ounces cream cheese, softened
4 tablespoons salted butter, softened
¼ cup firmly packed light brown sugar
¼ teaspoon vanilla extract

• In a small mixing bowl, beat together cream cheese, butter, brown sugar, and vanilla extract with a mixer at medium speed until light and creamy.

Maple Butter
Makes ½ cup

This sumptuous spread is perfect for our Bacon-Spelt Scones (page 74) and would be equally delightful on something as simple as toast.

½ cup salted butter, softened
2 teaspoons real maple syrup

• In a small bowl, stir together butter and maple syrup until well blended. Cover and refrigerate until needed, up to 5 days.

Honey Butter
Makes approximately ½ cup

Irresistible when spread on our Brie & Olive Scones (page 80), in particular, this honey-sweetened butter comes together effortlessly. Be sure to use European-style butter, which has a higher butterfat content than regular butter.

3½ ounces (approximately 7 tablespoons) salted
   European-style butter*, room temperature
1 teaspoon honey

• In a small bowl, beat together butter and honey with a mixer at medium speed until combined. Use immediately.

*We used Président butter.

Rosemary-Honey Butter

Makes 1 cup

This sweet and herbaceous spread is perfect for our Bacon-Butternut Gluten-Free Scones (page 120).

1 cup unsalted butter, softened
3 tablespoons honey
1 teaspoon dried rosemary
¼ teaspoon fine sea salt

• In a medium bowl, beat together butter, honey, rosemary, and salt with a mixer at medium speed until combined. Refrigerate for 15 minutes.
• Spoon butter mixture onto a sheet of parchment paper. Using parchment paper to help and wrap, shape butter mixture into a log. Refrigerate for at least 2 hours.
• To serve, unwrap butter and cut into ¼-inch-thick slices, using a warm, sharp knife.

Black Pepper Butter Rosettes

Makes ½ cup

This simple, yet delicious, recipe combines two household ingredients into a picture-perfect rosette, well suited to grace our Kalamata Olive–Rosemary Scones (page 81).

½ cup salted butter, softened
½ teaspoon coarsely ground black pepper*

• Line a rimmed baking sheet with wax paper.
• In a small bowl, stir together butter and pepper. Transfer butter to a piping bag fitted with a very large open-star tip (Ateco #847). Pipe rosettes of butter onto prepared baking sheet. Place baking sheet in freezer until butter freezes, approximately 4 hours.
• Just before serving, lift butter rosettes from wax paper, using an offset spatula.

*If using finely ground black pepper, reduce amount to ¼ teaspoon.

KITCHEN TIP: Butter rosettes can be transferred to an airtight container for longer freezer storage.

Golden Kiwi Jam

Makes approximately 2 cups

The Gold Kiwi is a patented variety naturally bred in New Zealand and has a sweeter taste than the original fruit.

4 large Gold Kiwis, peeled and quartered
1 cup granulated sugar
¼ cup water
2 teaspoons fresh lemon juice

• In a small saucepan, combine kiwis, sugar, ¼ cup water, and lemon juice. Bring to a boil over medium-high heat. Reduce heat to low, and let mixture simmer, uncovered, stirring frequently, until mixture thickens, 15 to 20 minutes. Remove from heat.
• Using a potato masher, mash kiwi mixture until slightly chunky. Let cool completely before transferring to an airtight container. Refrigerate until needed, up to a week.

Spiced Pear Compote

Makes 1 cup

Flavored with fresh ginger, cinnamon, cardamom, and Bartlett pears, this warm and fruity spread is absolutely delightful, especially when served along with our Vanilla Bean Scones (page 19).

¼ cup water
¼ cup granulated sugar
2 teaspoons sliced fresh ginger root
1 cinnamon stick
1 bay leaf
½ teaspoon whole cloves
¼ teaspoon fennel seed
¼ teaspoon black peppercorns
⅛ teaspoon ground cardamom
1 tablespoon salted butter
2 teaspoons light brown sugar
2 cups chopped, peeled Bartlett pears

• In a small saucepan, combine ¼ cup water, granulated sugar, ginger root, cinnamon stick, bay leaf, cloves, fennel seed, peppercorns, and cardamom. Bring just to a boil, stirring until sugar melts. Remove from heat, cover, and let steep for 15 minutes. Strain through a fine-mesh sieve, discarding solids. Reserve spiced syrup.
• In a skillet, cook together butter and brown sugar over medium heat, stirring until brown sugar melts.

Add pears, and gently toss to coat with butter mixture. Cook over low heat for 2 to 3 minutes. Add reserved spiced syrup, stirring to combine. Cook until pears are soft and tender and mixture has thickened, approximately 5 minutes. Serve warm.

MAKE-AHEAD TIP: *Spiced Pear Compote can be made a day in advance, covered, and refrigerated. Warm gently over low heat before serving.*

Lemon Curd
Makes approximately 1½ cups

This classic condiment is a beloved favorite, and you can't go wrong with this user-friendly, delicious recipe.

3 large eggs, lightly whisked
3 large egg yolks
1 cup plus 2 tablespoons granulated sugar
2 tablespoons fresh lemon zest
1 cup plus 2 tablespoons fresh lemon juice

• In a medium bowl, lightly whisk together eggs and egg yolks.
• In the top of a double boiler* over simmering water, whisk together sugar, lemon zest, lemon juice, and egg mixture until blended. Cook until thickened, approximately 20 minutes, stirring often.
• Remove from heat and strain curd** through a fine-mesh sieve into a heatproof, non-metal container. Cover top of curd with plastic wrap to prevent curd

from forming a skin while cooling. Let cool to room temperature. Refrigerate until cold. Store in an airtight container in the refrigerator and use within 2 weeks.

If a double boiler is not available, set a heatproof bowl over a pan of simmering water, making sure water does not touch bowl.
**For a shinier curd, whisk in 2 tablespoons butter, 1 tablespoon at a time, while curd is still hot.*

Strawberry-Raspberry Quick Jam
Makes 1½ cups

Fresh strawberries, raspberries, and oranges combine to create this delightfully fruity and oh-so-easy jam.

2½ cups sliced fresh strawberries
1 cup fresh raspberries
½ cup granulated sugar
1 tablespoon fresh orange zest
½ cup fresh orange juice

• In a medium saucepan, combine strawberries, raspberries, sugar, orange zest, and orange juice. Bring to a boil over medium-high heat, stirring frequently. Reduce heat to low, and cook, stirring frequently, until mixture thickens, approximately 30 minutes.
• Pour jam into a heatproof bowl, and place bowl in a larger bowl filled with crushed ice. Let jam cool, stirring occasionally.
• Transfer jam to a covered container, and refrigerate for up to 3 weeks, or freeze for up to 1 year.

SCONE-MAKING *How-to*

Let these step-by-step photos serve as your visual guide while you create
these impressive and delicious teatime treats.

1

In a large bowl, combine the dry ingredients, whisking well.

2

Using a pastry blender or 2 forks, cut butter into flour mixture until it resembles coarse crumbs.

3

If the recipe calls for dried fruit, nuts, chocolate, or other additions, add them at this point, tossing to combine.

4

Add wet ingredients to flour mixture, stirring until a shaggy dough begins to form.

5

Working gently, bring mixture together with hands until a dough forms. (If dough won't come together, add more liquid, 1 tablespoon at a time, until it does.)

6

Turn out dough onto a lightly floured surface, and knead gently until smooth by patting dough and folding it in half several times.

7

Using a rolling pin, roll out dough to thickness indicated in recipe, usually ½ to 1 inch.

8

Using a cutter dipped in flour, cut scones from dough without twisting cutter. Place scones on a parchment paper–lined baking sheet.

9

If the recipe calls for it, brush tops of scones with cream or another liquid. Bake according to recipe.

MAKE-AHEAD TIP: *Raw scones can be frozen completely on baking sheet and then transferred to an airtight freezer bag. Bake frozen scones without thawing, according to recipe directions, within 3 months.*

Acknowledgments

EDITOR Lorna Reeves
ART DIRECTOR Leighann Lott Bryant
ASSOCIATE EDITOR Katherine Ellis
COPY EDITOR Kellie Keeling
EDITORIAL ASSISTANT Shelby Duffy
CREATIVE DIRECTOR/PHOTOGRAPHY
Mac Jamieson
SENIOR PHOTOGRAPHER John O'Hagan
PHOTOGRAPHERS
Jim Bathie, Stephanie Welbourne Steele
CONTRIBUTING PHOTOGRAPHERS
William Dickey, Marcy Black Simpson
SENIOR DIGITAL IMAGE SPECIALIST
Delisa McDaniel
DIGITAL IMAGE SPECIALIST Clark Densmore
TEST KITCHEN DIRECTOR Laura Crandall
FOOD STYLISTS/RECIPE DEVELOPERS
Katie Moon Dickerson, Kathleen Kanen,
Vanessa Rocchio
CONTRIBUTING FOOD STYLISTS/RECIPE
DEVELOPERS Janet Lambert, Megan Lankford,
Emily Loughran, Jade Sinacori, Irene Yeh

COVER

Photography by Jim Bathie
Styling by Courtni Bodiford
Food Styling by Katie Moon Dickerson
Herend *Printemps* teapot, footed cup and saucer set,
mini creamer, mini covered sugar pot, 2-tiered stand;
Gorham Silver *Buttercup* butter spreader and teaspoon*.
Heritage Lace *Heirloom* table topper, 641-628-4949,
heritagelace.com.

TITLE PAGE

Page 1: Royal Albert *Memory Lane* teapot, footed cup
and saucer set, creamer and sugar set with tray, and
large sandwich tray*.

MASTHEAD

Pages 3–4: Bernardaud *Venise* teapot and lid*.
Bernardaud *Venise* dinner plates; Bernardaud *Heloise*
salad plates and flat cup and saucer set from Bernardaud
Boutique, 212-725-0699, bernardaud.com/en/us.
Candlesticks courtesy of Maison de France Antiques,
205-699-6330. Flower arrangement by FlowerBuds,
205-970-3223, flowerbudsfloristbirmingham.com.

TABLE OF CONTENTS

Page 5: Minton *Ancestral Gold* salad plate and flat cup
and saucer set; Minton *Chevron* dinner plate; Minton
Marlow Gold square cake plate*. Oneida *Golden Michelangelo*
20-piece flatware set from Oneida, oneida.com.

INTRODUCTION

Page 8: Noritake *Limerick* dinner plate, footed cup
and saucer set, sugar bowl, and 2-tiered serving tray;
Noritake *Palace Christmas Platinum* Holiday salad plate*.

TEA-STEEPING GUIDE

Page 9: Herend *Printemps* teapot, footed cup and saucer
set, mini creamer, mini covered sugar pot, and salad
plate*. Heritage Lace *Heirloom* table topper, 641-628-4949, heritagelace.com.

TEA-PAIRING GUIDE

Page 12: Haviland *Rosalinde* flat cup and saucer set, dinner
plate, and salad plate; Richard Ginori *Lime Green* charger*.

PLAIN SCONES

Pages 13 & 15: Wedgwood *Appledore* teapot and
5-piece place setting; Kirk Stieff *King* sterling silver tea

knife, individual salad fork, and teaspoon*. **Page 16:**
Small scalloped pedestal from Rosanna, 877-343-3779,
rosannainc.com. Scalloped white bowls from Pier 1,
pier1.com. Wedgwood *Columbia Gold* teapot*. **Page 17:**
Bernardaud *Venise* dinner plates; Bernardaud *Heloise*
salad plates and flat cup and saucer set from Bernardaud
Boutique, 212-725-0699, bernardaud.com/en/us. **Page 18:**
Lenox *Federal Cobalt Platinum* 5-piece place setting*.
Page 19: Richard Ginori *Siena Rust* scalloped salad
plate*. **Page 20:** Spode *Dimity* salad plate and 8-inch
oval vegetable bowl*. Colclough *6751* square salad plates
available for rent at Tea and Old Roses, 205-413-7753,
teaandoldroses.com. **Page 21:** Royal Copenhagen *Star
Fluted Christmas* 22-cm dish from Royal Copenhagen,
800-431-1992, royalcopenhagen.us. Kim Seybert *Fez* place
mat, 212-564-7850, kimseybert.com. Juliska *Isabella Clear*
3-inch round bowl; Wallace Silver *Grande Baroque* round
bowl soup spoon*. **Page 22:** Spode *Fleur De Lis–Gold*
5-piece place setting*. **Page 23:** Royal Albert *Canterbury*
dinner plate, bread and butter plate; Royal Worcester
Regency Ruby salad plate, cup and saucer set, and covered
sugar bowl*. Flower arrangement by FlowerBuds,
205-970-3223, flowerbudsfloristbirmingham.com. **Page 24:**
Herend *Silk Ribbon Fern* dessert plate; *Gwendolyn*
covered sugar and creamer from Herend, 800-643-7363,
herendusa.com. Kim Seybert *Harlequin Plum* place mats
from Kim Seybert, 212-564-7850, kimseybert.com.

SWEET SCONES

Page 25: Herend *Printemps* teapot, footed cup and
saucer set, salad plate, and 8-inch leaf dish; Gorham
Silver *Buttercup* butter spreader *. Heritage Lace
Heirloom table topper, 641-628-4949, heritagelace.com.
Page 27: Royal Crown Derby *Derby Panel Green* dinner
plate, salad plate, and footed cup and saucer set;
William Smiley *1WS1* (sterling holloware) 6-piece
silver tea set; Carrs *Victorian Bead* knife, salad fork,
and teaspoon*. Heritage Lace *Victorian Rose White* lace
overlay, 641-628-4949, heritagelace.com. Linen
hemstitch napkins and table runner in Cactus from
Pottery Barn, 888-779-5176, potterybarn.com. **Page 28:**
Grace's Teaware *Blue Butterfly* square salad/dessert plate;
Pink Butterfly sugar bowl*. **Page 29:** Kate Spade *Mercer
Drive* 5-piece place setting from Lenox, 800-223-4311,
lenox.com. Navy-and-ivory striped knit fabric from
Hobby Lobby, 800-888-0321, hobbylobby.com. Fish-
shaped condiment bowls from HomeGoods, 800-888-
0776, homegoods.com. **Page 32:** Two-tiered stand from
World Market, 877-967-5362, worldmarket.com. Oneida
Golden Michelangelo 20-piece flatware set from Oneida,
oneida.com. **Page 33:** Minton *Ancestral Gold* teapot,
salad plate, and flat cup and saucer set; Minton
Chevron dinner plate; Minton *Marlow Gold* 12-inch oval
serving platter and square cake plate*. Oneida *Golden
Michelangelo* 20-piece flatware set from Oneida,
oneida.com. **Page 34:** Royal Crown Derby *Carlton Red*
salad plate; Royal Doulton *Pacific* dinner plate*. Red
ruffle place mat from Pier 1 Imports, 817-252-6300,
pier1.com. Blue condiment bowl from Anthropologie,
800-309-2500, anthropologie.com. **Page 35:** Godinger
Dublin 3-tier serving rack from Godinger, 718-418-
1000, godinger.com. **Page 36:** Gien *Millefleurs* 5-piece
place setting from FX Dougherty, 800-834-3797,
fxdougherty.com. Skyros Designs *Linho* linen runner
from Bromberg's, 205-871-3276, brombergs.com.
Page 37: Rosetti *Spring Violets* footed cup and saucer
set; Hammersley *Victorian Violets* bon bon dish, jam/
jelly jar*. **Page 38:** Mottahedeh *Blue Lace* service plate;
Fostoria June *Topaz-Yellow* water goblet and small fruit/
dessert bowl; Ceralene *Blue Carnation* teapot and round
compote*. Seybert East West white and citron napkins

set of 4 from Kim Seybert, 212-564-7850, kimseybert.com.
Page 39: Noritake *Crestwood Cobalt Platinum*
5-piece place setting and sugar bowl with lid*.
Page 40: Mottahedeh *Duke of Gloucester* cup and saucer
set and oval platter from Mottahedeh, 800-443-8225,
mottahedeh.com. **Page 41:** Wedgwood *Golden Grosgrain*
5-piece place setting*. **Page 42:** Wedgwood *Hibiscus*
dinner plate, salad plate, teapot, and, teacup and saucer
set from Wedgwood, 877-720-3486, wedgwood.com.
Crystal salt/pepper dish (for condiments) from Chelsea
Antiques, 205-678-2151, chelseaantiques1.com. **Page 43:**
Royal Copenhagen *Blue Fluted Half Lace Border* 8-inch
square vegetable bowl; Royal Copenhagen *Blue Fluted
Full Lace* salad plate and butter pat; Royal Copenhagen
Princess Blue large dinner plate*. **Page 44:** Ellgreave
0482 teapot; Royal Grafton *881* creamer and sugar set;
Fieldings *Devon Ware* dinner plates; Minton *Minuet*
salad plates available for rent at Tea and Old Roses,
205-413-7753, teaandoldroses.com. **Page 45:** Shelley
Hedgerow teapot; Gorham *King Edward* demi spoon;
Federal Glass *Sharon Pink* vegetable bowl*. Green
tablecloth and napkin set from Hoover Antique Gallery,
205-822-9500, hooverantiquegalleryal.com. **Page 46:**
Royal Albert *Moonlight Rose* 3-tiered serving tray*.
Page 47: Haviland *Rosalinde* 5-piece place setting*.
Page 48: Royal Albert *Memory Lane* 5-piece place setting,
creamer and sugar set with tray, and large sandwich tray*.
Page 49: Herend *Printemps* teapot, footed cup and saucer
set, bread and butter plate, and 8-inch leaf dish; Gorham
Silver *Buttercup* butter spreader*. Heritage Lace *Heirloom*
table topper, 641-628-4949, heritagelace.com. **Page 50:**
Ceralene *La Fayette* octagonal luncheon plate, flat cup
and saucer set, 6-inch melon bowl; Wallace Silver *Grande
Baroque* youth knife, youth fork, youth 5 o'clock spoon,
and demitasse spoon*. April Cornell *Annalouise* tablecloth
from April Cornell, 888-332-7745, aprilcornell.com. Lace
trim pink chambray napkin from Pier 1, 888-384-0700,
pier1com. **Page 51:** Royal Albert *Enchantment* salad plate
and handled cake plate*. **Page 52:** Herend *Fish Scales*
raspberry bread and butter plate from Herend, 800-643-
7363, herendusa.com. Revol miniature heart dish from
Sur La Table, 800-243-0852, surlatable.com. **Page 53:**
Waterford *Lismore Lace Gold* china from Waterford,
877-720- 3485, waterford.com. Kim Seybert *Nomad*
napkins and *Bamboo* napkins rings from Kim Seybert,
212-564-7850, kimseybert.com. **Page 54:** Gien *Paris*
oblong tray and dessert/salad plate; Gien *Filet Taupe*
dinner plates and teacups/saucers from Yvonne Estelle's,
847-518-1232, yvonne-estelles.com. Tablecloth from
Red and White Kitchen Company, 877-914-7440,
redandwhitekitchen.com. **Page 56:** Spode *Blue Italian*
bread and butter plates and handled basket; Spode *Judaica*
square serving dish from Spode, 888-778-1471, spode.com.
Page 57: Rosanna Rachel Ashwell *The Prairie* tablecloth
from HomeGoods, 800-888-0776, homegoods.com.
Jadeite buffet napkins from World Market, 877-967-
5362, worldmarket.com. **Page 58:** Kate Spade *Library
Lane* round serving bowl and fruit bowls*. **Page 59:**
Villeroy & Boch *Toy's Delight* bread and butter plate,
salad plate, and dip bowl set with tray*. **Page 60:** Royal
Doulton *Rondo* bread and butter plate*. **Page 61:** Lenox
Vintage Jewel 2-tiered server; Opal *Innocence Scroll Gold*
place setting from Lenox, 800-223-4311, lenox.com.
Waterford *Octavia* tablecloth from Bed, Bath & Beyond,
800-462-3966, bedbathandbeyond.com. Silver condiment
bowls from World Market, 877-967-5362, worldmarket.com.
Page 62: Wedgwood *Pashmina* bread and butter
plate*. Annieglass *Roman Antique* mini bowl from
Bromberg's, 205-871-3276, brombergs.com. **Page 63:**
Mackenzie-Childs *Evergreen* enamel dinner plate,
salad/dessert plate, and compote (discontinued) from

Mackenzie-Childs, 888-665-1999, *mackenzie-childs.com*. Mackenzie-Childs *Courtly Check* enamel teacup and saucer from Christine's on Canterbury, 205-871-8297. **Page 64:** Wedgwood *Bianca* 10-inch oval vegetable bowl; Mitterteich *Golden Lark* dinner plate and footed cup and saucer set*. Condiment bowl from Anthropologie, 800-309-2500, *anthropologie.com*. White eyelet table runner from HomeGoods, 800-888-0776, *homegoods.com*. **Page 65:** Haviland *Autumn* vegetable bowl; George Jensen-Denmark *Acorn* knife butter spreader*. **Page 66:** Royal Crown Derby *Vine Gold* teacup and 10-inch oval vegetable bowl; *Vine Cobalt Blue* dinner plate; *Beaumont* embossed Sheffield dessert plate*. Gold chargers and *Mateo* cotton napkins from Pier 1, 888-384-0700, *pier1.com*. **Page 67:** Royal Copenhagen *Golden Basket* bread and butter plate*. Laura Ashley *Lace Scroll* tablecloth from HomeGoods, 800-888-0776, *homegoods.com*. **Page 68:** Lenox *French Pearle Bead White* dinner plate from Lenox, 800-223-4311, *lenox.com*. *Tava* flatware caddy in Espresso Stain from Pottery Barn, 888-779-5176, *potterybarn.com*. **Page 69:** Royal Albert *Brigadoon* salad plate*. **Page 70:** Arte Italica *Merletto Antique* salad/dessert plate and flat cup and saucer set; Arte Italica *Perlina* dinner plate; International Silver *Litchfield Pewter* flatware*. Bella Notte *Homespun White* napkin; Match Pewter *Queen Anne* oval bowl from Bromberg's, 205-871-3276, *brombergs.com*. Seeded eucalyptus garland from Pacific Garland, 503-207-6755, *pacificgarland.com*. Two-part condiment dish from At Home Furnishings, 205-879-3510, *athome-furnishings.com*.

SAVORY SCONES

Page 71: Paul Muller *The Autumn* teapot, salad plate, and 10-inch oval vegetable bowl*. **Page 74:** Herend *Livia* 5-piece place setting from Herend, 800-643-7363, *herendusa.com*. Leeber *Golden Vine* hammered spreader from Bromberg's, 205-871-3276, *brombergs.com*. Juliska *Isabella Clear* 3-inch round bowl*. **Page 75:** Royal Doulton *Belmont* salad plate; Gorham Silver *909-910* mini sterling creamer and open sugar bowl; Seltmann *Anita* teapot*. Oneida *Golden Michelangelo* dinner plate from Oneida, *oneida.com*. **Page 76:** Vera Wang *Grosgrain Indigo* 5-piece place setting from Wedgwood, 877-720-3486, *wedgwood.com*. **Page 77:** Hen House Linens *Lattice Work* napkin from Hen House Linens, 877-717-3595, *henhouselinens.com*. **Page 78:** Lenox *Marchesa Empire Pearl-Indigo* 5-piece place setting from Lenox, 800-223-4311, *lenox.com*. **Page 79:** Johnson Brothers *Old British Castles* flat cup and saucer set, salad plate, and condiment dish*. Tiered metal server from Pottery Barn, 888-779-5176, *potterybarn.com*. **Page 80:** Bernardaud *Capucine* dinner plate and butter pat; Bernardaud *Prunus* salad plate and bread and butter plate from Bernardaud, 212-725-0699, *bernardaud.com/en/us*. **Page 81:** Wedgwood *Columbia Black* bread and butter plate, salad plate, and footed cup and saucer set; Wedgwood *Colonnade Black* dinner plate*. **Page 82:** Lenox *Opal Innocence* dinner plate, bread and butter plate, and footed cup and saucer set; *Westmore* accent plate from Lenox, 800-223-4311, *lenox.com*. **Page 83:** Haviland *Imperatrice Eugenie* 6-inch pierced footed basket; Wedgwood *Ulander Gold* dinner plate*. **Page 84:** Paragon *First Love* oval vegetable bowl*. **Page 85:** Annieglass *Ruffle* oval platter from Annieglass, 800-347-6133, *annieglass.com*. **Page 86:** Sferra *Festival* napkin in Sunset from Sferra, 877-336-2003, *sferra.com*. **Page 87:** Schumann *Chateau Dresden* accent plate and pierced round bowl; Herend *Princess Victoria Green* dinner plate; Wallace *La Reine* silver flatware*. **Page 89:** Wedgwood *Geo Gold* charger, 5-piece place setting, and accent teapot from Wedgwood, 877-720-3486,

wedgwood.com. **Page 90:** Paul Muller *The Autumn* teacup and saucer set and 10-inch oval vegetable bowl*.

ALLERGY-FRIENDLY SCONES

Page 91: Noritake *Limerick* dinner plate, footed cup and saucer set, covered sugar bowl, and 2-tiered serving tray; Noritake *Palace Christmas Platinum* Holiday salad plate*. **Page 93:** Staffordshire *Calico Blue* salad plate, flat cup and saucer, and teapot*. **Page 94:** Crown Imperial *CIM9* dinner plate; Hutschenreuther *Sylvia* large dinner plate; Pope Gosser *Largo* bread and butter plate*. Heritage Lace *Canterbury* classic table topper, 641-628-4949, *heritagelace.com*. **Page 95:** Lenox *Winter Greetings* bread and butter plate*. **Page 96:** Lenox *Williamsburg Boxwood & Pine* dinner plate, accent luncheon plate, salad/dessert plate, flat cup and saucer set, and teapot*. **Page 97:** Royal Limoges *Margaux Gold* salad plate, teacup, and saucer from Bromberg's, 205-871-3276, *brombergs.com*. **Page 98:** Robert Haviland & C. Parlon *Sultane* dessert plate, teacup, and saucer from Bromberg's, 205-871-3276, *brombergs.com*. **Page 99:** Aynsley *Garden Gate* platter available for rent at Tea and Old Roses, 205-413-7753, *teaandoldroses.com*. Hammersley *Bridal Rose* footed cup and saucer set*. Lavender mini shiny latte bowl from Anthropologie, 800-309-2500, *anthropologie.com*. Grace Teaware silverplated teapot demi spoon from Gracie China Shop, *graciechinashop.com*. **Page 100:** Mottahedeh *Blue Lace* plate; Arcopal *Glenwood* salad plate; Johnson Brothers *Denmark Blue* dinner plate*. **Page 101:** Wedgwood *Geo Gold* bread and butter plate from Wedgwood, 877-720-3486, *wedgwood.com*. Royal Chelsea *RCH2* dinner plate and teacup and saucer set available for rent from Tea and Old Roses, 205-413-7753, *teaandoldroses.com*. **Page 102:** Grace's Teaware pedestal stand from HomeGoods, 800-888-0776, *homegoods.com*. White condiment bowls from Pier 1, 800-245-4595, *pier1.com*. Aynsley *Pembroke* teacup and saucer set and teapot*. **Page 103:** Johnson Brothers *Autumn Delight* bread and butter plate*. Vietri orange linen napkins from Bromberg's, 205-871-3276, *brombergs.com*. **Page 104:** Royal Stafford *Christmas Tree Red* salad plate; Royal Winton *Christmas Chintz* flat cup and saucer set*. **Page 105:** Vietri *Foglia* stone footed serving bowl from Bromberg's, 205-871-3276, *brombergs.com*. Condiment bowls from West Elm, 888-922-4119, *westelm.com*. AVA Style napkin from HomeGoods, 800-888-0776, *homegoods.com*. **Page 106:** Royal Crown Derby *Chelsea Duet* dinner plate; Haviland *Couronne Impériale White* dessert plate; William Yeoward *Crystal Pearl* champagne coupe from Bromberg's, 205-871-3276, *brombergs.com*. **Page 107:** Threshold *Wellsbridge Aqua* dinner plate; Mikasa *Wedding Band Gold* salad plate; Shelley *Marguerite* footed cup and saucer set*. FORLIFE *Dew* teapot with basket infuser from FORLIFE, 310-638-6386, *forlifedesignusa.com*. INUP Home Fine Linens table runner from HomeGoods, 800-888-0776, *homegoods.com*. **Page 108:** Mikasa *Parchment Rouge* dinner plate; *Holiday Traditions* footed cup and saucer set from Mikasa, 866-645-2721, *mikasa.com*. Henry Alcock *Manhattan Green* salad plate*. **Page 109:** Juliska *Country Estate* hostess tray from Bromberg's, 205-871-3276, *brombergs.com*. **Page 110:** Noritake *Limerick* dinner plate and 2-tiered serving tray; Noritake *Palace Christmas Platinum* holiday salad plate*. **Page 111:** American Atelier *Tradition* salad plate; Lenox *Judaic Blessings* metal menorah; Grace's Teaware *Metallic Gold Dots* teapot*. Herend *Golden Laurel* dinner plate and Royal Limoges *Danielle* dinner plate from Bromberg's, 205-871-3276, *brombergs.com*. **Page 112:** Herend *Fish Scale (Rust)* dessert plate; *Chinese Bouquet (Rust)* covered sugar with rose and creamer from Herend,

800-643-7363, *herendusa.com*. **Page 114:** Mikasa *Holiday Traditions* 5-piece place setting from Mikasa, 866-645-2721, *mikasa.com*. Juliska *Isabella Clear* 3-inch round bowl*. **Page 115:** Johnson Brothers *Fruit Sampler* footed cup and saucer set; Mason's *Friarswood* flat cup and saucer set*. **Page 116:** Juliska *Forest Walk* napkin from Bromberg's, 205-871-3276, *brombergs.com*. **Page 118:** Richard Ginori *Siena Rust* scalloped salad plate, dinner plate, and flat cup and saucer set*. **Page 119:** Kent Pottery teapot; Primo'gi pink basket from HomeGoods, 800-888-0776, *homegoods.com*. Royal Tara *Glendalough* footed cup and set*.

SPREADS

Page 122: Wedgwood *Bianca* salad plate and 10-inch oval vegetable bowl*. **Page 123: [Top]** Royal Copenhagen *Star Fluted Christmas* 22-cm dish from Royal Copenhagen, 800-431-1992, *royalcopenhagen.us*. Kim Seybert *Fez* place mat, 212-564-7850, *kimseybert.com*. Juliska *Isabella Clear* 3-inch round bowl; Wallace Silver *Grande Baroque* round bowl soup spoon*. **[Bottom]** Herend *Fish Scale (Rust)* dessert plate; *Chinese Bouquet (Rust)* covered sugar with rose and creamer from Herend, 800-643-7363, *herendusa.com*. **Page 125: [Top]** Noritake *Crestwood Cobalt Platinum* bread and butter plate*. **[Middle]** Herend *Livia* bread and butter plate from Herend, 800-643-7363, *herendusa.com*. Leeber *Golden Vine* hammered spreader from Bromberg's, 205-871-3276, *brombergs.com*. **[Bottom]** Bernardaud *Capucine* butter pat and dinner plate; Bernardaud *Prunus* salad plate and bread and butter plate from Bernardaud, 212-725-0699, *bernardaud.com/en/us*. **Page 126: [Bottom]** Wedgwood *Columbia Black* bread and butter plate and salad plate; Wedgwood *Colonnade Black* dinner plate*. **Page 127: [Top]** Haviland *Imperatrice Eugenie* salad plate; Wedgwood *Ulander Gold* dinner plate*. **[Bottom]** Juliska *Isabella Clear* 3-inch round bowl; Richard Ginori *Siena Rust* scalloped salad plate*. **Page 128: [Left]** Threshold *Wellsbridge Aqua* dinner plate; Mikasa *Wedding Band Gold* salad plate*.

BACK COVER

Photography by Jim Bathie
Styling by Courtni Bodiford
Food Styling by Megan Lankford
Haviland *Imperatrice Eugenie* 6-inch pierced footed basket; Wedgwood *Ulander Gold* dinner plate*.

* *from Replacements, Ltd., 800-737-5223, replacements.com.*

EDITOR'S NOTE: All items not listed are from private collections and no further information is available. Antique salt cellars (procured at antiques stores and estate sales) were used as personal-size condiment bowls in many of the photographs.

NOTABLE TEA PURVEYORS
• The Boulder Tea Company, 303-817-7057, *boulderteaco.com*
• Elmwood Inn Fine Teas, 800-765-2139, *elmwoodinn.com*
• Grace Tea Company, 978-635-9500, *gracetea.com*
• Harney & Sons, 888-427-6398, *harney.com*
• Mark T. Wendell Tea Company, 978-635-9200, *marktwendell.com*
• Simpson & Vail, 800-282-8327, *svtea.com*
• The Tea Shoppe, 304-413-0890, *theteashoppewv.com*

Recipe Index

EDITOR'S NOTE: Recipe titles shown in gold are gluten-free, provided gluten-free versions of processed ingredients (such as flours and extracts) are used.